MW01590831

Within Our Own Hearts

Twelve Dhamma Talks on Meditation Practice

by

Ayyā Khemā

Buddhist Publication Society
Kandy   Sri Lanka

Buddhist Publication Society
P.O. Box 61
54 Sangharaja Mawatha
Kandy, Sri Lanka
http://www.bps.lk

First edition: 1988
BPS edition: 2006
Published with the kind permission of Jhana Verlag.

National Library of Sri Lanka - Cataloguing in
Publication Data

Within our own hearts - Twelve Dhamma Talks on
  Meditation Practice - Ayyā Khemā - Kandy Buddhist
  Publication Society Inc., 2006 (BP 518S) 134p; 18cm
  ISBN-10: 955-24-0290-5
  ISBN-13: 978-955-24-0290-6   Price:
  i. 294.34435 DDC 21   ii. Title
  1. Meditation

Cover art: Martha Aitchison
Typeset at the BPS in the Palatino_BPS font

Printed in Sri Lanka by Ruchira Offset Printers
Kandy, Sri Lanka

BPS Publication BP 518S

Contents

Note to the First BPS Edition

A limited, private edition of this booklet was published in Sri Lanka in 1988. It has not been reprinted since.

In this new edition the original title *Little Dust in Our Eyes* has been changed to *Within Our Own Hearts* and the order of the first few chapters was altered.

We would like to express our gratitude to Jhana Verlag, Germany, which kindly granted us permission to reprint this work.

The Editor

Preface

A feeling seems to pervade intelligent people everywhere that conditions in the world are deteriorating drastically, so that peace loving neighbours are finding it hard not to be drawn into difficult and fearful situations.

It was the Buddha's explicit teaching that real peace and happiness cannot be found within worldly conditions. First, they are always changing, but also they do not contain enough depth and profundity to really satisfy the yearning in our hearts for a deep and lasting contentment.

This little volume of Dhamma talks is offered here to show a way out of our problems and suffering, to give an idea of the Buddha's way to reach ultimate peace and happiness. If anyone becomes inspired to practise this path of moral conduct, meditation and insight, our world will be so much the better for it.

Sister Ayyā Khemā

Chapter 1

The Seed of Enlightenment Within

There is only one place where enlightenment is possible, namely, in the mind. All of us have the seed of enlightenment within. If that were not so, there would be no point in leading a spiritual life. But since the potential *is* in all of us, it is wise to cultivate that seed.

If we have seeds for our garden and cultivate them, we have the chance of a harvest. We will water the garden, pull out the weeds and watch that the insects do not attack our plants. We keep an eye on the garden to see that everything is in good order. If there were no seeds it would be foolish to cultivate the plot. However hard we work, we would never see results. But since there are seeds, there is a chance of getting fruit. The same is true of our minds, yet we also have all the necessary weeds within to continue living in the world of duality, in the realm of birth and death. The weeds are our wrong thinking, based on the premise of our personal likes and dislikes. We approach people, experiences, situations with the view of gaining from them in some form. But how can we always expect to be given what we want?

Neither people nor situations nor experiences can be looked at in this way. They just are. Whether they are of benefit to ourselves or not, whether they enhance our egos or not, what difference can it make? Our mind with its luxurious growth of "craving to exist" approaches everything from the standpoint "what's in it for me?" This creates constant disappointment until we change our attitude.

We have a mind in which saṃsāra and Nibbāna can be found just as both happiness and unhappiness are present. It's almost like going to a department store and picking out what one wants. Why not pick that which is beneficial? If we go to a shop and buy everything we cannot use, that's rather foolish, isn't it? And at the same time, in the same place they are selling everything we need; so why not get that? Everything we need for our own and others' happiness is to be found in our own mind. Although all is available, people again and again pick that which has no benefit, for the simple reason that most people have neither heard about nor trained themselves to make mental and emotional choices. If we couldn't learn to make choices there would be no point in meditating. If everything was predestined, frozen into a pattern long before it happens, that would be fatalism. The Buddha described that as wrong view. If it were true, one could find no reason for being a truthful, decent person. One would not even find a reason for getting up in the morning, but could just as well stay in bed. We do have choices however. We can get up in the morning or stay in bed. We can tell ourselves that early morning is a good time for meditation, or we can say to ourselves how silly it is to get up early and prefer to stay in bed. We can convince ourselves either way. That's a choice, isn't it? We can see that we have choices under all circumstances.

There may be powerful situations arising where someone is abusive, stealing, threatening to kill or to defame. One believes oneself to be justified in feeling despondent about that. Why? One can choose and need not be forced to feel unhappy. We can recognize our potential to change our mind. The more often we choose a wholesome reaction, such as equanimity or loving-kindness, the more habitually the mind will be happy. The more wrong choices we make, the more often the mind will revert to unhappiness. The more anger we allow ourselves, the more geared towards anger our mind becomes. It's really quite simple; just a matter of creating the proper habit patterns in our mind. This then facilitates meditation which opens the door to break through the ego delusion.

Although we know about our ego delusion this understanding may not really have taken a hold yet. There is a great difference between knowledge and experience. As long as one is still trying to find a foothold somewhere in the world—whether it be wealth, fame, friendship, knowledge, understanding or anything else—one will he threatened by adversity. What is it that everybody is looking for? Only one thing—happiness. We want beautiful sights and sounds, pleasant tastes and comforts. But can these really continuously be experienced or can there be a kind of happiness which does not rely on our senses? An inner voice may whisper that happiness is actually based on purity and that unhappiness is a defilement. When one has a first inkling of that, there is amazement and often rejection. Most people find themselves unhappy quite often and don't want to admit to such a large measure of defilements. But how could being unhappy be a virtue? If we feel unhappy about others' suffering, there is only one way to deal with that, namely to help alleviate the suffering if we can. Otherwise such unhappiness results in emotionalism which clouds clear thinking.

When the Ven. Ānanda was standing crying at the deathbed of the Buddha, the Buddha reprimanded him. It was a sign that the Ven. Ānanda was not enlightened, had not yet relinquished craving. The Buddha said to Ven. Ānanda: "Come Ānanda; what are you crying about? Are you crying because this old body is finally breaking up?" Ven. Ānanda replied: "I am crying because my teacher is leaving me."

Unhappiness arises because there is resistance and rejection, which is craving to get rid of things as they are. Resistance and rejection are part of anger because nothing will ever be exactly as we wish. If we are still looking for satisfaction in worldly matters, we haven't seen Dhamma (the Truth) yet. That doesn't mean, however, that we have to find dissatisfaction. Actually, there is neither the one nor the other. There is eating, drinking, sleeping, and digesting, talking, being silent, looking, hearing, tasting, smelling, touching and thinking. What else is there? Where can we find satisfaction or dissatisfaction? There is nothing to be found; everything just is.

Being born and dying doesn't just mean our birth and death anniversaries, but rather that our thoughts and feelings are born and die from moment to moment. That's all we can find in this human realm. If we look for total irrevocable satisfaction, we won't find it, but to be dissatisfied is just as unskilful. What we have to look for is underlying absolute reality, *paramattha-dhamma*, that which shows itself as having no personality, no identity.

How will we find that? It we get concentrated in meditation, we may, at one point, know only awareness. At that moment we can experience that there is nothing in this world that can be added on to us, nor is there anything that can be taken away. The only reason we know about this is because there is awareness which can be placed wherever we like. We can, this moment, put our awareness into our home, and think: "I'd like to be there. All my friends are there." Wherever our awareness goes, that's where our thoughts will go.

So why not put our awareness on the fact that this world is empty of anything that has significance? We need not put our awareness on: "I am going to find something that will make me totally happy," because all of us have tried that without success. We are all intelligent people, yet nobody has found ultimate worldly happiness, always believing to have made some sort of mistake. But if we put our awareness on the underlying reality that there is nothing in this world which contains anything of substance, we may actually find ultimate happiness. Within the constant movement of birth and death, of arising and ceasing, there is no solid point that one can hang onto.

There is also the realization that fulfillment cannot come from outside but has to originate within, so that one doesn't look for anything worth knowing, owning or possessing. That can be experienced for a moment in one's meditation when one becomes aware of a pause between the breaths or between the thoughts; an awareness arises that there is nothing, only awareness.

Nothing. Why not put the attention on that? The mind will say: "Nothing? Maybe I can yet find something. I am still looking and don't want to come back empty handed." The stars, moon, sun, clouds, dogs, cats, birds, fish, lotus flowers, what will it be? People, children, grown-ups? Uncles, mothers, fathers? Whom can we select to bring us perfection? We can start from that premise and search, rather than assuming if we tackled it correctly, we would find the ultimate in worldly conditions.

Dukkha (unsatisfactoriness) goes away when one doesn't want anything, when there is nothing to be found that's worth having. When dukkha goes away, no choice needs to be made because then our inner department store is selling only one kind of goods, namely happiness and peacefulness. But when there are still happiness and unhappiness available, we must realize that the latter is due to resistance; either not getting what we want or getting what we don't want; not having things in the world in accordance with our own ideas or still hanging our happiness on a star out there. Sometimes we think happiness may be embedded in some mysterious person we haven't yet met. How can any other person experiencing dukkha, lacking core substance, ever bring us happiness? Just as everything in nature arises, gets born and dies, such as trees, birds, cats and flowers, we are exactly the same. Although we can talk about it, there is absolutely no difference between us and them. It is our inflated sense of ego which proclaims that we are the cream of the crop, the apex of creation.

Because we can reason, we believe we are different. But if we could really reason properly, why would we be unhappy, even for a moment? That's not very reasonable, is it? We have to come to that understanding through the meditative process, which will show us that the mind does not have to carry this ballast around. As long as the mind is burdened by likes and dislikes, it will experience dukkha. It is like a porter carrying a lot of luggage which is really heavy. As we are used to that, we think that's the way it has to be. In meditation we can experience moments of utter lightness, no burdens at all. Why then carry that baggage in daily living? It is not necessary to have it along, since it doesn't contain anything of value. More little suitcases filled with bricks! If it were of any value, then it would be a great pity that we are constantly losing all our thoughts and can hardly ever recapture them.

If we experience one single moment of lightness in our meditation, where none of this mental baggage is burdening us, surely that gives enough impetus to continue. Feeling inner lightness and no projections into the future or clinging to the past will then be our source of contentment.

Ambapāli was a prostitute in the Buddha's time and Aṅgulimāla was a murderer; both became enlightened. If they had clung to the past, they could never have achieved freedom.

People cling fast to less weighty subjects. They cling to what somebody said, or what they replied, what they did or didn't do. The human theatre is absurd! Why do we do all this? There can only be one answer. If we have no happiness with which to support the ego, then we must at least support it with unhappiness, without projecting into the future, or hanging onto the past, we can actually be without any mental burdens. When we drop all these thoughts for a moment, we realize that we were engaged in a totally unnecessary, exhausting mental exercise.

If we have the choice of carrying hundred pound weights in each hand and walking around with them, day in and day out, or of putting them down, what would we do? We would choose to be without them, wouldn't we? We have that choice in the mind too. Meditation teaches us that choice. If we know that unhappiness is a defilement, then every time it arises we can say to ourselves: "There is something wrong with my approach to this matter." Check unhappiness out against craving and letting go of that; you will be one of the rarest people in the world: one who is always happy.

Chapter 2

Nothing Special

Spiritual practice is often misunderstood and believed to be something special. It isn't. It is one's whole body and mind. Nothing special at all, just oneself. Many people think of it as meditation or ritual, devotional practice or chanting to be performed at a specific time in a certain place. Or it may be connected with a special person without whom the practice cannot occur. These are views and opinions which lead to nothing.

In the best case they may result in sporadic practice and in the worst case, they lead to fracturing ourselves, making two, three or four people out of ourselves when we aren't even one whole yet. Namely, the ordinary person doing all the ordinary worldly chores and the other one who becomes spiritual at certain times in diverse ways. Meditation, rituals, devotional practice, chanting, certain places, certain people can all be added to our lives, but they are not the essence of our spirituality.

Our practice consists of constant purification; there's nothing else to be done. Eventually we will arrive at a point where our thought processes and feelings are not only kind and loving but also full of wisdom, bringing benefit to ourselves and others.

That is possibly a designation of a goal. In order to get to that goal, however, we need to know exactly where we stand; otherwise how can we start on this journey? Many people go around in circles in their spiritual practice, either having exaggerated or underrated ideas of their own worth. Both are detrimental to a fundamental recognition of ourselves.

We need to inquire into any discomfort arising within. Imagine you are sitting on a pillow with one leg bent in such a way that the discomfort becomes greater and greater. Would you do something about it or would you just keep sitting like that for the rest of your life? Physical discomfort is something that all of us wish to escape from or alleviate, and discard as quickly as possible. What about mental and emotional discomfort?

What can be compared in importance to that and why do we feel uncomfortable so often? Nobody feels at ease in an untidy, messy household, or likewise when there are unwholesome aspects arising in our inner household such as resistances, dislikes, fears, feeling threatened, worries about our past or future. How can that be comfortable?

Only when we realize that we are the manufacturers of our own discomforts is there any opening for change. If we still believe that other people, situations or the lack of appreciation, praise, love or opportunities, are at fault, we haven't started our practice yet.

We must arrive at a starting point. If one runs a race, one has to find the starting line. We have to find a point of departure for this practice which is found within our own inner being. Only those people who are determined to grow in spirituality will find that fundamental basis within, from which inner growth can be generated.

The whole person becomes involved and not just for the few hours of meditation or scattered moments of remembrance. The whole of each of us working the whole time at it can become purified.

There must be no lip-service; it has to be real. All discomfort within us, all unhappiness, fear or worry, have been created by ourselves. Only then is the field wide open for change. That moment of acceptance and realization changes our whole world because now we can do something about our lives. Until then we were helpless victims. We cannot change the world or other people; we can hardly even change the behaviour of a dog, but we can change ourselves. As long as we only believe this, but don't do it, we haven't started to practise. We can even sit in meditation, but no results will show in our lives.

It starts with inner softness, acceptance and pliability. We become open to people and situations around us. If we retain our own ideas and viewpoints, continually liking or disliking the same areas of life, we are not sensitive to our inner reactions. Softness, acceptance and sensitivity may result in a great deal of pain, but that's part of practice. However, because it's painful, it's often rejected. Surely, that is the wrong way of dealing with ourselves. If we break a leg and don't want to have it set because that is painful, it would mean limping for the rest of our lives. This is equivalent to looking for a lifelong anaesthetic, which dulls all awareness and keeps us in a semi-awake state.

Because all of us have the six roots of greed, hate and delusion and their opposites of generosity, love and wisdom, we are constantly manifesting one of these. Love and hate, greed and generosity are usually equally distributed in most people. Delusion, however, is the underlying factor of all our mental emotional activities, and wisdom is rare. We are not actually hating anyone because he is hateful, but rather because our inner hate is looking for an outlet. This is one of the great absurdities of humanity, and only a very few people are aware of this simple fact which could change our whole life. When we hate, we don't do so because there's anything worth hating or disliking but only because hate wants to manifest itself.

The one who becomes unhappy in the first instance is the one who hates. This negative emotion is like a barb, which we would like to use to hurt others, but first pricks the one who is holding on to it. This is a law of nature and so simple that most people overlook it completely. We go through life having a distinct demarcation line: on the right everything we like and on the left everything we dislike. Certain qualities and characteristics are always either good or bad in our opinion. Sometimes it does not work out quite that way and we hate to shift our demarcation line. It's not a comfortable way of living. One is a person who cannot be happy because it's impossible to find only people and things that one likes. Since there is no perfection in existence, there's no hope for happiness in such a mode of reacting. It is amazing that most people have not woken up to this fact. Many have spoken and written about it but it remains a matter of spiritual practice.

To recapitulate: first, we know that we are the doer. We are responsible for whatever is arising within us. Second, we can change because we realize that the dislikes, hates, fears and worries are creating unhappiness for ourselves.

Change necessitates substitution. Here we can appreciate the training in meditation, where we are constantly called upon to substitute our thinking with being attentive to the breath. For one who doesn't meditate the substitution of one thought for another is an unknown factor. To exchange all unwholesome thought with a wholesome thought is an almost unbelievable idea for people who do not know anything about spiritual practice. We are prone to believe what we are thinking.

That nobody else is thinking the same has never occurred to us. To be the only one with such a thought amongst four billion inhabitants is an absurdity rarely noticed.

The next important step in our maturing process is the recognition of our own dukkha. This seems so simple that one wonders why it is often difficult to follow through with it. If we have dukkha, like everybody does, we are in the first instance inclined to blame someone or something. We can start with people, continue with situations, and include our sense contacts, what we hear, see, taste, touch and smell. The possibilities for blame are infinite. But when we indulge in them, we are refusing our first insight; namely, that we ourselves are responsible. If we hold fast to that understanding, then we begin to see dukkha in a different way. Namely, as part and parcel of being human; as a universal and not a personal truth. However, when we are disliking our painful feelings and are not willing to accept the fact that our own mind is the culprit, then we will look for a scapegoat. This is a very popular past-time and possible scapegoats are innumerable. When we remember that we're causing our own dukkha, we are back to spiritual practice. As we dislike our own dukkha, hate arises at the same time which results in "double dukkha."

Using insight into self-made dukkha as our next step, we have a chance of changing the discomfort within ourselves from dislike and hate to, at least, acceptance. Eventually a feeling of being at ease with oneself arises, without which meditation cannot flourish.

These are fundamental aspects of ourselves which we need to investigate and experience. Spiritual practice involves one's whole being and the exploration of our reactions, developing sensitivity and vulnerability to others and being able to roll with the punches. We begin to realize that there are certain necessary learning situations in our lives and if we don't make use of them, we will get the same ones over and over again. If we look back for a moment, we may be able to see identical situations having arisen many times. They'll continue to do so many lifetimes, unless we change.

Spiritual practice is not just sitting on a pillow but more an opening of the mind to what is actually going on inside. If that opening is closed the moment we stand up, then we haven't really been meditating successfully. It is not so much how long we can attend to the breath or the sensations but rather how aware and awake we become. Then we can use that awareness in our everyday reactions and thinking processes. There is the Cartesian view: "I think, therefore I am." Actually it's the other way around: "I am, therefore I think." Unless we can get some kind of order into our thoughts and emotional reactions which follow the thinking process, our mind will constantly play havoc with our inner household.

The realization of where our dukkha comes from must be followed by the understanding that disliking it will not make it go away; only letting go of wanting makes dukkha disappear, which means unequivocal acceptance. Accepting oneself results in being able to accept others. The difficulty with other people is that they present a mirror in which we can see our own mistakes. How useful it is to have such a mirror. When we live with others we can see ourselves as if it were a mirror-image and eventually we learn to be together like milk with water which completely blend. It is up to each one of us to blend, if we wait for others to do it we are not practising. This is a difficult undertaking, but also a very important one. Eventually we will create the inner comfort to expand our consciousness and awareness to universality.

The world at large is very busy and we get caught up in extraneous matters. The world inside is also very busy, but we can do something about that. We can quieten it down to see more clearly. The way of spiritual practice is nothing special, just our whole body and mind.

Chapter 3

Role Playing

"All the world's a stage,
And all the men and women merely players,"

wrote Shakespeare. The Buddha would have approved of Shakespeare's words.

We can take this statement a little farther and imagine that we are famous actresses with important roles. Maybe one time we play the Queen in *A Midsummer Night's Dream* or another time Gretchen in *Faust* or Macbeth's wife and try to do a very good job in each role. Before we get on stage we put on the appropriate costume in the dressing room and then go out to say our lines as well as we can. We may get some applause and are quite happy. When we get back to the dressing room, we put on our street clothes and go home. We don't still believe we are Macbeth's wife—do we? Or the Queen in *A Midsummer Night's Dream* or Gretchen? We are whoever we were when we left home.

During a career of twenty or thirty years we might be playing innumerable different roles. Just think for a moment, how many roles you have played in this life. Daughter, sister, student, friend, lover, mother-these are just a few of them. Secretary, book-keeper, gardener, cook and bottle-washer, nursemaid—so many different roles. Every time you might have been putting on a different costume too; you don't wear the same outfit to the office that you wear while cooking or gardening at home. Different roles, different costumes! The problem, however, arises when we believe that we are the one who is playing the role. When the actress goes home, she is still Kathryn Hepburn or whatever her name may be. But every time we play a different role in this lifetime, we believe ourselves to be that person and identify with it. Because of this belief, we don't realize that it is only a guest performance that ends the moment we stop doing what is required of that role. Instead, we continue to create the image of ourselves in all these roles, which is quite absurd. One can't be a gardener from early morning till late at night and while we are sleeping we don't even remember who we were during the preceding day.

Our identification process makes attachments arise, not necessarily to one particular role, but to being somebody with some significance. We think: "I am a wife and mother, a doctor or lawyer, because I am acting in the appropriate manner." Just imagine for a moment you were back on stage, an actress, performing in a play. Surely, you aren't really the person whom you are portraying. It's just a role, isn't it?

Our attachment arises from believing that we are one complete identity. If we are unhappy, we think we can change our role and "be" someone else. If being a wife doesn't bring joy, one can be a divorcee; or if being a nun doesn't make one happy, one can be a beach-girl instead. If that doesn't work either, then maybe "being" an Indian sādhu will be successful. Every time one of the roles doesn't bring fulfilment we are apt to try a new one, by putting on new clothes and using a new backdrop. Just think for a moment how many roles we play in a single day. One moment we are students, another instance we serve meals, another hour and we are leaders. Each time it appears to be "me," and so "I" look for approval. If the applause from the audience isn't forthcoming— sometimes the act just doesn't turn out that well—there is misery.

It is a human phenomenon that we know this and yet don't act accordingly, because it's too difficult to do so. It's actually much easier not to identify with one's role, because then one need not wait for the applause. If it's only a role and not "me," then it doesn't matter whether anybody is applauding the performance. We try our best, but that is all. Even if somebody should throw rotten tomatoes it would not matter, since it's only a stage play. This second aspect, which brings relief, is the lack of fear. Stage-fright of an actress is caused by self-consciousness; wanting to be liked and appreciated, and the fear that it may be otherwise. The same happens to us when we identify with our roles.

It is ignorance and self-delusion which prevent us from loosening our hold on the ownership of our roles. Habitual ways of thinking which have created patterns are blocking the way to a brand new inner vision. We need to stand back and realize that nothing is the way it appears to be. We are taking part in a play and anybody who ever believes in the show's absolute reality will always experience difficulties. The play finishes when the curtain goes down and that might happen at any moment. Then we have to wait for the next show to begin. Role playing, taken so seriously by everybody, arises out of attachment and creates stronger attachment, because when we believe that role to be "us" we get attached to it and because we are attached, we believe the role to be "us."

The body is the physical actor, and the mind says the appropriate lines. Sometimes one might say the wrong lines and that causes misery and disharmony. Just as in a play when somebody has forgotten his/her lines and the other person doesn't get the right cue, difficulties arise.

It is essential that one decides which role is the most useful one to eventually be pensioned off in, and be able to sit back and relax. If one changes one's costume again and again and gets a new role every time one is dissatisfied, surely one can not expect to come to an end of one's career. On the contrary, we'll be part of this theatre over and over again. Most people like that because it has entertainment value. But at times the entertainment ceases and suffering (*dukkha*) arises due to attachments. Anything that we believe to be "us" or to belong to "me," to be "me" or "mine" creates dukkha. But when we realize our guest status, we do not feel attached or burdened.

Imagine you are in a botanical garden and pretend you own the place. What a burden! How to keep all the flowering plants and trees alive, nurture them, manure them, pull the weeds out, and clean the paths. On the other hand, you have just bought a ten cent ticket and walked in to have a look at the garden. Wonderful, isn't it? Beautiful! A lovely afternoon spent in a botanical garden.

What about this body? We think we own it, don't we? What a burden! Doesn't this body create a lot of misery for us? But if we truly own the body, why doesn't it obey? Why doesn't it comply with our commands, never to have aches or pains, always to be wide awake, never to get old, sick or die? If, however, we are just a visitor in this body, then maybe all the unfortunate things that happen to it aren't quite as important.

When we visit the botanical gardens and see a tree with a lot of sickly, yellow leaves, we do not worry about the tree. It doesn't matter to us, does it? We just keep walking around the gardens, looking at the other trees. The same principle applies to this body and its sickness and eventual death. The most insidious role we are playing is "me and my body, me and my shadow." Practically everybody knows they don't own this body, yet almost no one lives accordingly. This body is the most demanding entity we are faced with. It has to be fed, cleaned, washed, nails, and hair cut. It has to eat, drink, go to the toilet, sleep, exercise, have its teeth fixed. There is no end to it. Often it needs rest.

If we consider our bodies to be guest-houses where we happen to visit for a while, there is nothing to get worried about. Our ownership delusion would automatically dissipate itself. All the role playing we do in this life would be seen for just what it is—nothing but this body acting another part, wearing an appropriate costume. In reality there is nobody wearing the outfit, only the thirty-two parts of the body holding it up.

These considerations are skilful means for detachment from owning our bodies, because of the realization that ownership brings nothing but misery—particularly owning a body which is never satisfied. Either it is too full or too empty, too hot or too cold. It sneezes because the wind comes up. It can't sit in comfort because it has been in one position too long, or it has been lying down too long and needs to sit up now. It can't do anything for a long time, not walking, running, sitting or lying down.

Yet it happens to be a useful guest-house and costume, a useful role for us as human beings. But we must not become attached to it. It's just as absurd to be attached to being a certain person as it is to be identified as Macbeth's wife.

We've all had many different roles in our innumerable past lives. We were infants, school children, then teenagers, university students, fathers, mothers, grandparents and in each role we thought of being that person, and through it finding some happiness. How can any role bring happiness?" Only when there is applause from the audience. But how can that happiness last? A few moments or even a day and then all is forgotten and has to be done over and over again. Isn't it interesting and amazing that four billion human beings are working and living for a little applause to make them happy! If someone doesn't applaud, support or affirm us, then we have dukkha because we think we aren't successful. Do check to see whether this is truly so in your own life. If this has been your experience, try to stand back far enough from your-self to get a new slant on the whole picture. One needs to be the right distance from a mirror to see one's true likeness.

Repeat performances are very boring. As long as we wear the blinkers of attachment and wrong views, we have what we might call tunnel vision. It would be very illuminating to see ourselves as others see us, totally detached, not "owning" or "being," just observing.

Everything we think we own creates fear, namely, the fear of loss. Furthermore, we are caught in guarding our property by repairing and dusting, repainting and replacing. None of the material things we own live up to our expectations, neither do the ideas and images we have of ourselves. We have to dust them off constantly and repair them. Our self-image is often splintered when others disapprove. Not to own anything no images no views about oneself, no attachment, no role is so much less worry, so much more peace.

We can just get on with practising not to come back for a repeat of a next life of playing innumerable roles. We can inquire: "Who am I really?" If the answer is "me," find out who "me" is. Which part is "me"? The one who is playing the role of the wife or the mother, the gardener or the Dhamma student? Which one is real? All of them? A whole crew of actors all rolled into one person. What a fantastic performance! We are all acting these different parts quite credibly because we believe them ourselves, and always hope that others will believe us too. That doesn't always work. Sometimes others don't believe us because they themselves have other views. We have to make this self-inquiry if we want to find out what work is to be done for our peace of mind.

What is our working ground? There is a hook that we are hanging on. We can find that hook and once we are off the hook, there are no problems. An alert, awake, intelligent mind can do it. The more our meditation practice flourishes, the more alert and awake the mind becomes and the more it is able to see, understand and accept a different vision. The meditative mind accepts that nothing is the way it looks, but is just an interesting play we are engaged in. If we are lucky, we may get a fair bit of applause. But who is being applauded? Which is our main role that we want to be applauded for? Even the Buddha didn't get only support and approval. There is always somebody who has opposing opinions. Is it really worthwhile trying for applause for any of our roles? Or is it better to see the temporary and fleeting nature of the whole performance and thereby attain peace and happiness based on that insight?

Chapter 4

Self-love, Self-hate

Self-love and self-hate are extreme emotions caused by our ego delusion and both are equally damaging.

Exaggerated self-love means that one has nobody else in mind except oneself. Whatever doesn't concern oneself isn't interesting. To some degree, everybody acts like this. But if taken to extremes, such people have little chance of practising a spiritual path. They will only listen if their own interests are at stake. These people are often lonely because they do not relate well to others whose affairs are of no personal concern to them. They are sitting within their cocoons, waiting to emerge as a beautiful butterfly, and don't want to know what is going on outside.

However, lack of self-love, which is equally common, also denotes too much self-interest. Instead of thinking "I am better than you," self-hate is caused by thinking "I am worse than you." The main difficulty lies in "I am."

Neither attitude brings peace of mind, nor a lessening of the ego concept, and both have self-consciousness as their result. Being very conscious of "self" makes life unnecessarily difficult.

Whenever a new situation arises, it presents an obstacle, because "self" is judging and evaluating the personal gain or loss. Either "I am not good enough to do this," or "I am much too good." If one doesn't feel as capable or as clever as other people, then there is dissatisfaction. A discontented person will project that state of mind as dissatisfaction with other people or one's situation in life.

Whatever we think and feel towards ourselves, we manifest towards others. Even though we would often like to disguise or hide our state of mind, it is impossible to do so. Reason and rationality tell us quite clearly that our reactions are often useless and often not even sensible. But reason and rationality do not prevail, while feeling does. We live according to our feelings; no matter how reasonable and intelligent we may be.

If we feel discontented and dissatisfied with ourselves, not feeling quite good enough, then we will feel the same about everybody else. This is a dangerous situation, not easy to live with, painful and sad. If we meet somebody who is suffering from physical pain, we are aware of that, aren't we? The person may be moaning, or gritting his teeth; he might not be able to respond in a normal way because there is so much physical discomfort. Do you think it is any different with mental pain? If we confront somebody who suffers from mental pain, we realize that also. Such inner discomfort can certainly not be hidden, but colours all personal relationships, whether they are

28

close or more distant ones. A person who experiences pain with every step he takes will probably try to take as few steps as possible and walk very carefully, so as not to aggravate the pain. The same happens with mental pain. To have self-hate and discontent with oneself is very painful for oneself and all those we meet and relate to.

We often have the illusion that we are kind and helpful, of service, and concerned with the well-being of others. Rationally and intellectually that may be so, since we all know that this is skilful action. But feelingly we have to work from the centre of our own heart and mind. Unless we have found a way of dealing skilfully with ourselves, how can we hope to reach others? How would we ever be able to relate to the postman if we are not yet at ease with ourselves? But let us deal with our own ego first in a way which creates the least disturbance for ourselves and for others.

Taking it easy is one extreme; never having done enough is the other, and neither one of them is desirable. The middle path of looking at oneself as if one were one's own mother is love coupled with wisdom. If we become our own mother and are at the same time our own difficult child, we may find the balance between self-love and self-hate. A sensible mother looks after her child with love and compassion, but also with gentle and consistent discipline. Most children don't like being disciplined, but a good mother knows the need to continue doing it. If we are both mother and child, we will realize that the child in us has to grow up and the mother in us helps the process. This creates neither indulgence nor discontent and obstruction. A sensible mother finds a difficult child a challenge and this is the challenge we all face, namely to bring ourselves to total maturity. Lack of love for, and discontent with her child is not the attitude of a mother, but rather, constant guidance over and over again.

Insight into the fact that one's own ego is the trouble-maker comes when we realize that the child in us wants its own way. We may feel quite motivated then to practise diligently to reach final liberation. But we find we have to see quite clearly that there is no other problem anywhere in the whole of the universe except our ego delusion. This wrong view of "self" brings about our cravings which, continually create dukkha for us, whether we want to be better or more capable, more enlightened or more peaceful, important or more appreciated. All "wants" are a result of discontent and a source of suffering. If the Buddha's teaching is to be realized, the first two noble truths have to be seen within oneself Namely, that it doesn't matter how exalted the wanting is, it is still dukkha. Only when we appreciate this fact for what it means to us, can we eventually let go.

We will never reach a state of non-self (*anatta*) if we don't get a grip on "self" first, and know it for the trouble-maker it is. Every time self-conceit arises and creates difficulties, we can learn to let go moment to moment. Yet the question remains: "Do I really want to get rid of 'self'? What have I got instead?" As long as we think there might be another way out of dukkha, even though we haven't found it yet, we will be ambivalent about practising wholeheartedly.

If we think of ourselves as mother and child, the child being guided and disciplined, there is a chance to see the ego games we play. Just as a mother loves her child, no matter what game it plays, no matter how many difficulties the child creates, the same applies to us. Whatever we do, love is the necessary ingredient in our lives. Whether we are lovable or not, is not the criteria. Only the Arahant is totally lovable; everybody else has egocentricity and self-interest. Love is the soft, warm feeling without which life doesn't flow. If we can't generate it towards ourselves, we won't be able to extend it to others, no matter how much we would like to do so. As much of that warmth as we have for ourselves, that's as much as we can give other beings.

Love is a quality of the heart without the discriminating faculty of the mind. If you have children of your own, you can extend the feeling you have for them to yourself. You have a mother whom you love, so you know the feeling she has for you, and that again will help you to realize how to deal with yourself. Every time we become aware of the difficulties that the ego creates for

31

us, we are a little nearer to the realization of "no-self" because we will be strengthened in our resolve to get rid of this trouble-maker. It's not enough to avoid or resolve problems. We have to eliminate the cause, otherwise difficulties will arise again and again.

Self-love, self-hate—two sides of the same coin. The answer lies in the middle where we can experience a feeling of security and of painless relationship to ourselves. If there is no hurt within ourselves, it is much easier to live with others. Start each day by giving yourself some loving warm feelings as if you were your own mother. It helps to settle the mind and attune it to the heart. Heart and mind have to be in harmony to make us whole. What we think and what we feel is so often miles apart because we use thoughts as a substitute for feeling. Bring heart and mind into tune with each other by releasing from your heart as much lovingness as you can towards yourself at the beginning of each day. Then create a joyful attitude in yourself because of this great opportunity of learning and growing which you have in this life. Look at yourself with the loving eyes of a mother and the wisdom that a mother has for the growth of her child.

Chapter 5

Training the Heart

At the time of the Buddha there lived a man called Kesi, who was a horse trainer. One day he went to the Buddha and said that in his business of training horses, he treated them in four ways. With a certain kind of horse, all he had to do was talk to it and direct it with his legs and the horse would obey. Then there was another kind of horse to whom he would have to show the whip, but he wouldn't have to use it. There was a third kind of horse on whom he'd actually have to use the whip to make it pay attention. But he'd also come across another kind of horse where all three methods failed. That horse was so useless that he would shoot it. He wanted the Buddha's opinion on that.

The Buddha replied: "I do exactly the same thing with my disciples."

Kesi was amazed. "You are a monk, a Buddha, an Enlightened One, a recluse, and you would do that? You would kill a disciple if he doesn't obey you?"

The Buddha said: "It's like this. There are certain disciples to whom I have to speak once and they understand—they are easy to train. There are also certain disciples to whom I have to tell that if they don't obey they are making bad kamma. If they hear it sufficiently often, they will finally learn. There are also those disciples on whom I have to impose discipline and tell them in very definite terms how they have to behave. Then they learn after some time. But there are also disciples where none of these three methods will work and those I shoot; I kill them." Kesi said: "I can't believe that. I have never heard that you were killing anybody."

The Buddha replied: "When I kill a disciple that means that I will not teach him or her anymore. As far as the Dhamma is concerned that disciple is dead. In that way I kill them. Because only when I teach them are they alive for the Dhamma and alive for me as a teacher." Kesi was satisfied and took his leave.

When we hear this story, we must also remember the last words of the Buddha: "Be islands unto yourselves, be refuges unto yourselves; practise with diligence." He often mentioned that people should follow the Dhamma, the teaching, and not him, the person. When we hear these words, we must not mistakenly think that the Dhamma exists in our hearts already without the teaching and the teacher. If that were so, we would all be enlightened already.

On the contrary, we need heart-felt gratitude that not only the teaching exists for us, but that there are also teachers able to expound it. Unless we make the best use of this opportunity, we might be killed. Because if we don't learn now, the Dhamma may not be alive for us later. If we don't use the present opportunity with all our might, then we are already dead inside of us. We lack the openness to accept something new and when, one isn't ready for change, one might as well be dead.

Hopefully, we would be disciples of the first kind. Those who need only to be told once and then realize the truth within: those disciples are rare. But there are some who easily understand what needs to be done, yet are not able to do it right away because defilements are still in the way. They realize that this purification process is essential; they can see their own defilements and accept the fact that patience and time will bring about a change. In the Buddha's time disciples were called *sāvakas*, which means "hearer," somebody who hears and listens. The Dhamma needs to be heard and practised to create a change in one's heart and mind.

There are many more people, who need the threat of bad kamma, of the hell realms, to be coerced into wholesome behaviour. This is being shown the whip. That is why the Buddha said: "Shame and fear are the guardians of the world." These people need the fear of punishment to spur them on. The Buddha mentions that the wise disciple is afraid to take a wrong step in thought, speech or action because such a disciple knows that would be for his/her own detriment.

Temptations are constantly arising. The Buddha was sitting under the Bodhi tree, just moments away from Enlightenment and temptation arose. The daughters of Māra (the tempter) tried to pull him away from his meditation seat. If temptation can arise in a person of such stature, accomplishment and achievements, we can understand how often we can be tempted into wrong thoughts, speech or action and can guard ourselves against them. Fear can arise that such unwholesomeness would create pain for oneself. Everyone has his temptations, his own defilements, looks after his own affairs. Each one is busy with himself. So whom can I hurt? Only myself. The idea of the foolishness of hurting oneself may arise. Obviously, ordinary people do make mistakes; but how can one train an untrained horse? By repeating the same lesson over and over again.

A horse trainer has to be very skilful. I don't know if any of you have ever come across an unbroken horse. They run all over the place, do whatever they like and get themselves into all sorts of trouble. In fact, they sometimes actually kill themselves by falling down gullies and breaking their legs. A horse trainer has to repeat his instructions over and over again to protect himself and the horse. But as you can see from the Buddha's story, there is a limit to that repetition.

If we belong to the most common kind of people, we would be afraid to do wrong and the more afraid we are, the less we would be tempted. That doesn't mean that we are afraid of other people, the teacher, the Dhamma or anything wholesome. We are only afraid of our own defilements and we try to minimise them. We see them in ourselves, not as our enemies, but as our challengers. They are saying: "Are you going to fall into this trap or aren't you? Are you going to get rid of me or not?"

It's not useful to become depressed about our own defilements as this is just another negativity. The only thing to do with a defilement is to realize its existence and use it as a challenge. If life didn't have any challenges, it would get very boring. That's why we should try to learn something new every day to challenge our thought, speech and reaction patterns. When we don't do that, we get so set in our ways that we can't change anymore.

If we are not the kind of people who are afraid to do wrong, then fear has to be instilled in us. That's why the Buddha talked about the whip that might be used. He had disciples who behaved so badly that he scolded and admonished them severely. He had to make rule after rule, so that we have a Vinaya (rules of discipline) of five volumes. The fear of punishment is the whip.

Once, when the misbehaviour of the monks was extreme, the Buddha went into the forest and said: "I've taught my disciples whatever I know, but some are unteachable." "The story goes that an elephant and a monkey brought him his daily meal in the form of mangoes and bananas. After three months of this, the lay people begged the Buddha to come back because the other monks were not able to teach them as skilfully as the Buddha himself.

When all else failed, the Buddha would actually sever a monk from having communication with the rest of the Sangha and would not teach him any longer. That happened to poor Channa, who redeemed himself in the end. Channa had a way of getting the other monks angry by pretending to be a special companion of the Buddha. When the Buddha was still Prince Siddhartha, Channa had been his charioteer. He developed the habit of saying "our Buddha" or "my Buddha" and "our Sangha" or "my Sangha" as if he and the Buddha together had established the Sangha and as if the Buddha was more "his" than anyone else's. Instead of practising meditation, he riled everybody with his manner of talking and wouldn't listen to any of the elder monks who could have been his teachers. Finally, the Buddha imposed a high penalty on him: having no communication with any other monk. This so shocked Channa that he soon attained Arahantship.

The Buddha penalized Channa because he could see no other way of training him, and also to protect the other monks from mental strain. This was equivalent to killing his disciple, by no longer heeding him.

A teacher has to use appropriate methods to teach different people. One time a western yogi came to Ajahn Chah who is a well known meditation teacher in north-east Thailand. He said to him: "Sir, I am confused and don't know any more what's right or wrong. Sometimes you tell one of your disciples to do one thing and then I hear you tell someone else the complete opposite. What am I to believe? " Ajahn Chah replied: "If I see a car on the highway constantly veering to the right and in danger of falling into the ditch on the right, I am certainly going to advise the driver to swerve left. However, if I see a car constantly veering to the left, in danger of falling into the left ditch, I am going to tell the driver to move to the right. That way I can save both from disaster, yet one has to move to the left and one has to move right."

One person might need encouragement and support in his difficulties and another person might need to be told to be quiet and introspect. The only consistency we can find is the need to work on eliminating our defilements. The more we keep them with us, the more we hurt ourselves. Purification of thought, speech and action is the prescription. The medicine is the supreme effort to get our thoughts into the right grooves and channels and thereby good speech and actions will follow. It would be well to be the kind of disciple that is afraid of doing the wrong thing because of hurting his growth towards spiritual emancipation.

If we have no fear of wrong doing, our development will be curtailed and in the end we will kill ourselves—not physically of course—but mentally and emotionally. Since nothing remains the same, but all constantly changes, we are either going forward or backward in our maturing process, but we never can remain in one spot. The only person of any consequence in this effort is oneself. Everybody else is the scenery or the "field of merit." We can earn merit by being kind, considerate and be helpful to others, yet our defilements are waiting for our personal attention.

We need to become skilful at living. We may think we know how to live, just because we are alive. But how many people are really skilful at that? When we have trained our hearts and minds to be at peace, then joy arises within. Our own difficulties became minor, so that we have ample opportunity to be helpful towards others. When we have that kind of skill, then we are actually living proof of the Buddha's Dhamma.

Chapter 6

Abandon What Should Be Abandoned

The *āsavas* are deeply embedded cravings which usually escape our awareness. We take our delusions for granted because we know nothing else. Sometimes we have an inkling of them when our cravings run up against a barrier in someone else. But these underlying defilements are so deeply ingrained within us that we are not even sure that they exist until we start serious practice.

When our desires are not gratified, we either think that the other person is at fault or that there was a communication gap or that others are peculiar. But that the craving coming from us is met by the same thing in the other person is hard to realize until we have obtained strong mindfulness.

The first of our deeply ingrained desires is for sensual gratification. This is the greed inherent in us to have only pleasant experiences. Anyone who hasn't practised will say: "Why not? Why shouldn't I want it pleasant?" The reason is that we cannot rely on having pleasant sense contacts and failing to get them, unhappiness ensues. Even when one does get them, they cannot last. It's a foregone conclusion that it is a losing battle which the whole world is engaged in, yet impossible to win. All of us are trying to get what we want because we have craving embedded within us based on illusion that this is "me" and "I" want pleasant feelings. If we think about it for a moment, what else do we want?

The second trait is our "craving-to-be." We don't want to be killed or annihilated or diminished. We want to be here and as comfortable as possible. The third one is "ignorance," which is the foundation for all our difficulties because we are ignoring the fact that the other two cravings are impossible to gratify and that reality lies somewhere else.

These three desires flow out of every ordinary person. Everybody is beset by ignorance, craving for pleasant sensations and craving-to-be-here, which means being supported without any danger or fear. Everyone wants it at the expense of everyone else, and our other reactions are coloured by these desires. So we can understand why people have difficulty relating to one another. If we can realize, first of all, that these mind-states are creating problems and trouble for us, we can also accept that the craving to have pleasure and comfort cannot be permanently gratified. It surely is not a worthwhile goal to stake a whole human life on. When we consider our craving for existence, we can readily understand that it is a lost cause, since nobody survives. To stake one's life on survival is futile and foolish.

Yet, those two cravings underlie everything we do. If we can see for just a moment that they are not useful, then we will be interested to find out how to get rid of them. Most people cannot see any alternative and aren't aware of the fact that these mind-states cause all our unhappiness. Whether the unhappiness is called frustration, boredom, anger, worry, fear, envy or jealousy doesn't matter; all of them are based on those two cravings with ignorance as their underlying foundation.

If one has given enough consideration to the fact that one is saddled with such a problem and that one would be happier without it, the interest on how to abandon it arises. The Buddha gives very explicit instructions on how to go about that through:

1. Wise consideration
2. Subjugation
3. Right use
4. Endurance
5. Avoidance
6. Letting go
7. Cultivation

The first mode of conduct is "wise consideration." One puts one's mind in the direction where craving for sensual gratification does not necessarily arise or grow. We do not start to imagine what it would be like to take a trip on a luxury liner or to be swimming at the Riviera or to eat at an excellent restaurant, or couldn't it be cool outside instead of hot. Such imaginings create more craving for pleasant sensations. If the mind gets enough food of that nature, then it will eventually try to actualize these desires, which means a lot of energy output in that direction. Instead of giving the mind more cause for craving by thinking where it could get additional pleasurable contacts, we can give the mind the possibility to see the truth, such as the reality of dukkha (unsatisfactoriness). This will not create unhappiness, because dukkha is not a personal matter; dukkha is universal. Everybody has it; no one is singled out.

Naturally, we give our own dukkha a special name and special reasons. That's all imagination. There aren't any special causes or special dukkha. The cause is always the same, namely craving. Wise consideration is to look at all one's desires which are not being gratified or which are not yielding the expected pleasures and then realizing the unfulfilled craving in the mind. This is the direct experience of the truth of dukkha and of its cause, allowing for the third Noble Truth, that there is a way out. But it can't be found by getting everything one wants, nor by having more pleasures and comforts, more appreciation and praise, more ego support, but by letting go of wishes and desires.

The Buddha mentioned various unwise considerations, namely, about past and future lives, about having a self or having no self, or about being aware of myself or being aware of my non-self. All of that supports the ego illusion. Instead, we must consider the basic fact of unhappiness and that its arising is due to wanting something. The stronger our ego illusion, the more unhappiness we experience. Of course, it is very difficult to realize that because we don't know any other state of being and cannot imagine that other people could feel differently. We might think they are putting on a good show or are just lucky. But the truth of the matter is, the stronger the ego, the more one wants, the more dukkha. Quite simple, but difficult to practise. Wise consideration means that one constantly pulls one's mind back from all imaginations and ideations and places it firmly on the moment to moment reality. Considering dukkha objectively does not mean being full of dukkha but rather reflecting on it. One has an introspective attitude which is objective and sees things as they are, not as one would like them to be, which is unrealistic, wishful thinking. If one gains insight into the law of nature, then one day everything will be as one would like it, only different from the way one would have imagined.

There are six other ways of working towards the elimination of our deeply embedded taints, towards getting rid of one's ever recurring unhappiness. Not by trying to achieve happiness, but by letting go of ingrained habit patterns. They are all practice paths that will eventually result in

45

equanimity (even-mindedness) and a removal of the barriers to deep insight.

The first way is to become aware of the reaction to one's sense contacts. We make contact automatically through our six senses, and the ensuing feelings are also automatic, but our reaction to those feelings is arbitrary. Obviously, we will not constantly be able to stop reacting, but once in a while it is certainly possible. We can change ourselves by not reacting to a feeling, by not liking or disliking it. Then we are taking the first big step towards freedom from compulsion. This needs the objectivity of mindfulness and one's undivided attention. As one practises more and more, it becomes easier as all repetitions do. That's the way of subjugation recommended by the Buddha.

The next way is "right use." Everything we own should be something that we need. We should be very aware of the difference between a need and a want. The Buddha said there are only four items that one really needs—food, clothing, shelter and medicine. The rest are all extras. We can check to see whether we really make use of our possessions for the benefit of others or whether they are only kept to create pleasant feelings in ourselves. If the latter, it is best to give them away. It's good practice to check our belongings once a month and give unused items as gifts to others. It's not so much having nothing but rather having little. There is always the possibility of transforming one's belongings into the valuable

46

assets of other people. The main consideration is to know whether one would be able to give everything away at a moment's notice. Not to imagine that one could do it, but to start doing it immediately. When death hits us, we have to give up everything including ourselves. Life is uncertain, but death is completely certain—at any time. The right use of what one has means that one does not have a strong attachment to the things one owns; one is aware of the fact that they are only on loan. One knows that they are for the benefit of everyone and that there is no need to have more. This is another way again of seeing that pleasant sense contacts will not create real happiness. On the contrary, they will in the end create nothing but unhappiness.

In our affluent society pleasant sense contacts are as readily available as sand on the beach. Pleasant sense contacts can be had anywhere, any time; one just has to be able to pay for them. Yet how many people do we know who are truly happy? They can all get pleasant sense contacts over and over again and have probably been getting them all their lives. That's not the answer. The way to freedom includes "subjugation" and "right-use."

Another way is avoiding wrong company and wrong places; namely, where pleasant sense contacts are being bartered, where people have no interest in Dhamma. Wrong people are those who have no real yearning for spiritual growth. There

47

are many people in the world who think they are practising. They might sit in meditation, chant or offer flowers, read Dhamma books, have philosophical discussions, yet it remains on the surface. It is better than no interest at all, but it doesn't go to the depth of the problem; if it did, these people would by now have become very happy. Yet, when one inquires, they have just as many problems as anybody else. The truth has not penetrated their psyche. The taints are the deepest layer where one's whole being is felt. As long as our cravings are embedded in there, we are part of existence and that means dukkha.

Our third mode of transformation is avoidance of those contacts where sensual desire and pleasant sense contacts are the main issue. The world at large, not knowing that there are alternatives, considers these the most important. This is the underlying ignorance which gives rise to the wrong view of self. Subjugation of reacting to the pleasant sense contacts is one side of the coin; endurance, which is the enduring of the unpleasant sense contacts, is the other. When there is an unpleasant sensation, for instance in the sitting posture, and the body becomes very uncomfortable, it is good practice to endure. Nobody gets away during a lifetime without physical pain. Being able to endure means that one does not have to suffer because of such pain. The more often one can endure, the more disciplined the mind becomes. The untrained mind becomes turbulent every time there is something unpleasant that it doesn't like or something pleasant that it wants to keep. These waves in the mind are the irritations, the lack of peacefulness that everybody experiences. They cause a feeling of uneasiness and insecurity. Endurance can also be practised in the face of an emotional discomfort. To be able to endure is another way of getting away from reactions which mean diminishing craving.

Then there is removal: letting go, dropping. Whatever we are reacting to, whether it is with anger and grief, with wanting or rejecting, envy or pride, worry or fear, we need to recognise the reaction and drop it. Removal does not mean suppression. One cannot remove what one hasn't acknowledged first. This letting-go procedure is one of the most important aspects of spiritual maturing. The Buddha's teachings cannot make any impact unless one practises them. "Letting go" is not being attached, not owning what one thinks and feels. If one believes every thought and every feeling, if one is glued to them as the mind likes to be, then "letting go" is not possible. How can we let go of something that is utterly myself? If it is "me" thinking and feeling, how can we drop that? But when there is just a thought or a feeling and the objectivity of mindfulness points to its unwholesomeness or useless quality, "letting go" is possible. When we can drop desires, rejections and resistances, then we have started to practise.

The Buddha said that practice is not external but strictly internal. We can wear different clothes, shave off our hair, stay up all night, eat only one meal a day, but if there is no internal change, then these practices are done in vain. There has to be insight into oneself since all our desires are within. They are not in clothes or food or wakefulness. Removal, letting go, is the most important aspect of our work of purification. It applies equally to meditation. If we don't drop discursive thinking, we cannot meditate. When we say: "I've had a very bad meditation," it just means it wasn't possible to let go of the thoughts. They kept coming and going constantly. Letting go in daily life of unwholesome thoughts and emotions strengthens the meditation; learning the same in meditation helps one's daily life.

The last step is cultivation which applies to meditation, the cultivation of the mind, that process which eventually will result in the seven factors of enlightenment. Mindfulness is the first of these seven factors, and without it there can be no practice. Only the mind which has been cultivated has the strength and clarity to generate the factors of enlightenment and will also be the sort of mind willing to practise diligently, because constant alertness, awareness and self-examination are required. Only a clear and strong mind is willing and able to do that.

This brings about an investigation of all phenomena (*dhammas*), in view of their arising and ceasing, their essential impermanence. Everything that exists is a phenomenon; there is nothing else. If we examine in that way, then we are reflecting wisely. We can do that in the meditation practice as well as in daily living. In meditation, when the mind has become concentrated, it is essential to experience the arising of each mind moment and also the ceasing of it.

That investigation will help greatly to generate a calm mind which can see things in their true essence. When mindfulness and investigation have been practised in meditation so that they form a strong foundation, then subsequent factors will also arise which are tranquillity, joy and deep concentration. This will finally result in total equanimity. These are all necessary steps to be taken so that there is a path of practice which will not only improve meditation but will also change one's whole inner being. Certainly meditation has a great deal to do with that, but it's not all of it. There are also instant reactions and confrontations. Not only when other people are involved—even with trifles such as one's own meal. One is confronted with oneself being sleepy or hungry, being bored or discontented. If one doesn't use wisdom in these confrontations, then it remains difficult to see a different reality. If we use introspection in our daily experiences, our outlook changes.

This is a slow process, and as it takes place, the āsavas are diminished. They only disappear for an enlightened one (Arahant), but the outflow is gradually not as strong anymore. It resembles a flood in the beginning, later it may become a meandering stream, and then a trickle. The practice is to change the flood into a trickle, then it may completely dry out one day. Cultivation of the mind presupposes that we know that craving is to our detriment, as only then will we take the necessary steps towards inner peace.

Chapter 7

Where Can the Dust Alight?

Hui Neng was the sixth Zen Patriarch. When the fifth Zen Patriarch was getting old, he looked for a successor. He let it be known that he wanted every monk in his monastery to write a small essay or poem giving the essence of the Buddha's teaching. His favourite disciple and the one considered to be most advanced, took a piece of chalk and wrote on the wall:

> *Our body is the Bodhi-tree,*
> *And our mind is mirror bright.*
> *Carefully we wipe them hour by hour*
> *And let no dust alight.*

Hui-Neng was a young illiterate scullery boy at that time. He heard of the writing on the wall and asked someone to write beneath:

> *There is no Bodhi-tree;*
> *Nor stand of a mirror bright,*
> *Since all is void,*
> *Where can the dust alight?*

The teacher saw these two statements and declared Hui-Neng to be his successor. Hui-Neng, who had hardly received any instruction by then, later ordained as a monk and in time became a very famous Zen Master whose teachings are consolidated in the *Platform Sutta*.

The two statements above remind us of the Brahmajāla Sutta. Clearing the dust off the mirror is the purification of virtue. The clearing away of the dust of the defilements was the first disciple's concern. In the Brahmajāla Sutta, a worldling considered the Buddha's virtues and morality as his great achievement, but the Buddha said they were a trifling matter.

This is precisely what the Fifth Patriarch thought when he preferred Hui-Neng's statement over the first one. Certainly, there has to be virtue and purification. We have to clean the dust off the mirror of heart and mind, otherwise we can't see clearly. While this is a true statement, it is not the essence of the teaching; it's only the beginning. The Buddha said: "It is a trifling matter, a small thing and only a worldling would praise me for that." Only someone who hasn't personally seen Nibbāna would make this point. This shows us that the disciple who formulated the first sentence about cleaning the dust off the mirror was a worldling who hadn't seen Nibbāna. Otherwise, he wouldn't have specified this as the essence of the teaching. It is nothing but the cleaning-up process, although that certainly is important. We don't just clean kuṭis and pathways, white clothes and robes, meditation halls and bathrooms, we also clean our hearts and minds. It is a vital preliminary step.

"If all is void, where can the dust alight?" After the Buddha had described in the Brahmajāla Sutta all the wrong views people have, for instance, eternalist or annihilationist views (sixty-two wrong views in all), he again and again explained that a liberated being neither hates the unpleasant feelings nor lusts after the pleasant ones. This means that as long as there is a mirror, dust will inevitably settle on it; namely, as long as there is a "me" there will always be reactions. When we react to our feelings we know that we are worldlings. As long as there is any kind of reaction to feelings, the ego is catching the dust.

There are only two kinds of reactions, and they can be strong or mild. They are either wanting and enjoying the pleasant feelings or resisting and disliking the unpleasant ones. There can be strong reactions which are out of tune, such as becoming passionately involved with something pleasant, or likewise with something unpleasant. Crying, lamenting or getting angry about the one, or thinking, dreaming of nothing else except the other, hankering for some pleasant substitute if the desired one is denied.

The worldling who hasn't personally seen Nibbāna will react to feelings and because of ego-mirror the dust of desire will settle. Have you ever known a mirror not to get dirty? It isn't possible.

Such is the nature of the material universe, and the same applies to the spiritual universe. As long as there is a "me," it will have defilements. It cannot be any other way. That's why the Buddha's teaching shows the only way out of unhappiness, out of defilements, namely to lose the "me" delusion. As long as there is anything inside which says: "This is me," there have to be difficulties, dust and impurity. There is no mirror that doesn't collect dust, and there is no "me" that doesn't collect defilements. That's why the Buddha said: "My virtue is a trifling matter," and that's why the first disciple who said: "Clean off the dust," was not accepted as a Dhamma heir.

We can polish the mirror again and again, just as we sweep the kuṭis and pathways, cut the trees, take a shower and wash our clothes again and again, yet all will be dusty again and again. This is not the solution. The Buddha's solution is that of a genius, a spiritual giant. He is the only master who taught that the way to liberation is to get rid of the mirror. One can't keep the mirror clean anyway. So why keep the mirror? No one else ever thought of it in this way. He explained that it is quite possible to get rid of the mirror of the "me" because in reality it doesn't even exist, being a mind-made illusion.

In order to get rid of the idea of individualized personality, we have to keep looking at that aspect of ourselves again and again. As long as we believe that there is a mirror which we need to polish, we'll obviously keep on polishing it. It's the same as the Emperor's clothes. As long as we believe he is wearing them, we'll say: "Beautiful, beautiful." Only when we finally realize that in reality he has no clothes on at all, will we know the truth.[1]

If there is a mirror, we'll naturally want to clean it because it looks dirty, and that's as it should be. That's a worlding's practice of the spiritual life. Again and again we have to work on our reactions, on our passions, our rejections and resistances. They may diminish in strength and become less frequent, but they won't disappear. What we can lose, though, is the "me" delusion, and then there is nothing for the dust to settle on, nobody who can react, nothing to react to. That is a genius solution to the human problem; no other can compare.

To smash the mirror is obviously no way of getting nearer to the answer. When we smash a mirror, what do we get? Many bits and pieces, a mirror that we can't even look into anymore, with a lot of debris around. It's useless flitting at or cracking the "me," suppressing it or telling it to go away. Pretending that it isn't there is also a popular pastime which doesn't work, because as long as it exists, it will collect the dust, no matter

---

1 Ayyā Khemā is referring to Hans Christian Anderson's tale called *The Emporer's New Clothes*. (Editor)

how much we deny its existence. The pretence that it has vanished doesn't change anything.

What we can do is to use mindfulness coupled with investigation and introspection. "Who is acting, thinking or feeling?" When the answer "me" arises, then we can investigate who is this "me." Just because a thought occurred, we believe this to be "me." How come? Because we own the thought? Could we also disown the thought? Of course, we could. We could easily say: "I am not going to have that thought, I will have a different one." We are faced with the continual problem of hanging onto our feelings, thoughts and bodies and believe them to be "me." Through constant investigation that bondage can be loosened and we get some distance from "me" to enable us to reflect better.

As long as there is no space between "me" and "my" thoughts, we are right inside of them and can see practically nothing. It's the same as looking into a mirror. If we have our noses stuck against the mirror, we can't see a thing. We have to be the right distance from it for proper recognition. The more often we inquire into who is thinking, feeling, acting, the more the bondage of this tight ownership loosens. Then there is a space, and we can take an unobstructed look.

Our second line of approach is remembering, as part of mindfulness, that all is impermanent and fleeting. Every time a feeling arises that we are tempted to react to, we can look at the impermanence of it. Mindfulness means that we are objective and not involved. Besides non-reaction, we also need to be totally attentive to what is going on inside of ourselves. Even if we don't have a full understanding of the Dhamma, we can verify it through practice. The Buddha said mindfulness is the way to liberation so that we can eventually see quite clearly that:

> *There is the deed but no doer,*
> *there is suffering but no sufferer,*
> *there is the path but no one to enter it,*
> *there is Nibbāna but no one to attain it.*[2]

When there is an inkling in our mind about "no self," then we can expand on that, like a seed that we cultivate. If there is no seed, it is useless trying to work with it. When we get that first glimmer that the whole idea of "me" could be a delusion, then we can examine that over and over again, until it becomes more of a reality. Then we are on the way to losing wrong view about ourselves, which is the essence of the Dhamma.

When we see everything in the light of right view, it propels us along the path and keeps us practising. If we still have the conventional view about ourselves, as untrained minds do, then we easily slip off the path. Because it's "me" on the path and training isn't that comfortable; "I" could have a better time somewhere else. But right view doesn't allow for that

---

2 *Visuddhimagga* 16.90; trans. *The Path of Purification* (Ed.)

kind of confusion, because one knows there is nothing important except to continually let go of the mirror which collects the dust. Obviously, we can't get rid of the dust in any other way.

Anything that exists needs cleaning. Only when all is empty of substance is there no more cleaning to do. What a relief that would be! No cleaning at all, no washing, no sweeping, no reactions, just staying perfectly clean and still all the time. Nothing ever to worry about or to fear, nothing to feel guilty about or blame oneself for, nothing to regret and nothing to hope for either. Just as it is! As long as there is a mirror, it will collect the dust. When the mirror is gone, where can the dust settle?

Chapter 8

Spiritual Growth

Our meditation must have a direction. Otherwise we lose our way. Our direction is insight, which leads to liberation. How does one gain insight and how does one use it? Insight can be called an understood experience.

Every person, every living being, constantly has the experience of impermanence, but without fully understanding it there is no way to benefit from it. On the contrary, most people try to disguise impermanence, forget about it, or not acknowledge it. That holds true for practically everyone, because unless we fully grasp the significance of impermanence, we are denying it. When we do not pay complete attention, we don't have a relationship to it, so it is not part of our life.

There is no thought, feeling or bodily sensation, nor movement or action, nor any moment in any day that remains. All is constantly slipping away from us. Instead of using this very obvious happening which we are subject to all the time, and recognising its significance, we just let it go on without paying attention. The only time most of us become alert is when something very unpleasant has passed. How wonderful that there is impermanence then! But that is not the most opportune moment for realizing the changing nature of all phenomena. When something pleasant has disappeared from our lives is the time to notice how powerless we are in the grip of this relentless law of nature.

The experience of impermanence within ourselves has to be fully recognised so that a different attitude arises. Only then can we speak of insight. These inner changes through insight are not dramatic upheavals, but rather slow and gentle movements which in the long run amount to a complete turn-about.

An understood experience in meditation does not deal only with impermanence. There are other experiences equally valuable, but none can be termed insight if they don't result in an inner knowing and subsequent transformation. This understanding arises out of silent verbalization after the meditation is over. During meditation the experience takes place and afterwards one is able to realize its impact. Only then can we follow through with action.

Insight is true when we make use of it in our life. As an example, during meditation we may have had a clear vision of being the owner of our own kamma, being responsible for all that happens to us. At that moment it is an understood experience, but it will only bear fruit if we act upon it by resolving and following through with making as little bad kamma as possible from then on. In this manner spiritual growth takes place. Taking the meditative experience as one's trigger and then acting upon it as much and as often as mindfulness allows, will make the new insight part of our being. As that happens we change slowly into a different sort of person.

When such a change takes place, we may clearly realize that there is no constant being anywhere to be found, as the "me" known of old seems different now. This is what the spiritual life is all about: changing ourselves. At times we may see quite clearly that there is nobody who is a solid entity, that there is only action and reaction. Our understood experience will not appear to be of world shattering significance, but rather how to conduct ourselves in day to day living and how to practise the spiritual path.

Liberation from all dukkha comes through two different means—through the heart and through the mind. When we speak about liberation through the mind or wisdom, we refer to the understanding we gain through the direct experience of impermanence. When we speak about the liberation of the heart we speak about the opening of our feelings into an all embracing, never wavering love and compassion. Whichever pathway our insight leads us doesn't matter; the reason is certain pre-conditions which we have brought with us into this life.

To be fully open means that we hold nothing back, no views or opinions, pre-conceived notions or fears; just a total giving of ourselves to the experience on hand. Surely that needs practice and time, but each and every meditation contains experiences. Whether it is physical pain or boredom, whether it is dislike or tranquillity, rapture or resentment: something is bound to take place. If there was nothing at all happening, we would be sitting on the pillow like a vegetable.

If our negativities are understood as hindrances, not as personal calamities, then we need not react to them and will have gained insight at the same time. If positive experiences such as tranquillity, happiness or peacefulness are examined in the light of impermanence as being nothing but conditioned states which do not liberate, then again we have taken a leap into wisdom.

All states that are based on a condition have to be impermanent, since the condition, in this case concentration, does not last. Insight, however, remains with us and we can deepen our understanding through repetition.

All our previous thoughts, actions and reactions have created the personality we are. We have a tremendous job to let go of those deeply embedded mind-states which have been habitual for innumerable lifetimes. We can, however, recapture mind-states which contain our insights into absolute truth. As we repeat such thoughts as much and as often as possible, they will eventually become second nature to us. That means we have changed our nature and having done so, we are on the way to liberation—the greatest change of all.

Every single experience, in or out of meditation, can be used for understanding, but not in the way of worldly knowledge, rather in the way of spiritual truths. When we see everything that happens in the light of an underlying reality beyond worldly evaluations, we are changing our nature into the direction of spiritual growth. All happenings that form part of our daily life can then be seen as nothing but results arising from conditions prevalent in our mind continuum. They have no personality of their own, nor do we need to get involved with them. We can practise this in meditation, namely, that any kind of experience, any mind-state, any feeling, is looked at simply as a condition. This means that we see only phenomena, realizing their arising and ceasing, their unsatisfactory nature and their conditioned existence.

In the way of practice it is important to use both approaches, namely, the opening of the heart and the opening of the mind, because thereby we expand our opportunities. We have the mind that understands and the heart that feels. Understanding is gained through objective mindfulness and expansion of the heart through repeatedly caring and loving. Both ways together offer the best chance for growth because we are allowing ourselves to use all our faculties.

Even the most mundane experiences lend themselves to insight since mind and body are of this world, and they constitute our basis for introspection. We need not prefer one experience over another. Only when we became involved in what is happening without objectivity, then there is no gain for us. As long as we are wide awake and fully aware, we will learn the truth in all situations. Our starting point is exactly where we are now, and eventually we become what we already know. This may be the most difficult, but also the most rewarding experience of all.

Chapter 9

The Heart is the Base of Consciousness

The mind (*citta*) consists of feeling, perceptions, mental formations (thoughts) and sense consciousness, so that we are justified in calling it either "mind" or "heart." When we talk about consciousness, we often mean awareness. In the descriptive terminology of the Buddha we find the heart mentioned as the base of consciousness. This contradicts our usual belief that thinking is the foundation for our awareness. It makes feeling the lynchpin of all our experiences.

If our feelings are purified, loving, compassionate, helpful and generous, then such is the underlying consciousness from which we operate. Here is happiness in a nutshell, which depends entirely on our inner consciousness. We know that when we are angry, upset, anxious, or fearful, we cannot react calmly. Our awareness will not lend itself to peace and equanimity at such a time. It is a contradiction in terms and in inner direction.

As we train to master our emotions, we can open our awareness to happiness and peacefulness. However, we also have the choice to open ourselves to negative and sad states, worries, fears, and dislikes. It's the same mind that creates either positive or negative inner states and if we want to grow and mature, we need to consider emotional purification of prime importance. Emotional purity brings clarity of thinking and is therefore essential for wisdom. A fortunate factor in our consciousness is our inability to be aware of two different directions at the same time, so that we can train to be conscious of that which is helpful and valuable.

If we do not master this lesson, we will remain a victim of our emotions, which is not a very satisfactory way of living. We have to learn that negative emotions, as such, are nothing but the uncontrolled heart base. All dukkha means we are out of control. It is a very heartening aspect of the Buddha's teaching that it promises we can gain control over ourselves if we work at it.

The consciousness that is due to a purified heart base opens itself up to universal truths which surpass and transcend the pettiness of individual personality. We have heard and read that self or ego is a total delusion. But this remains another interesting piece of information to carry around in our heads, already full of assorted knowledge, most of it fairly useless. Although this information is not useless, as long as it remains information, it does not have a great deal of significance. If we purify our heart base and open ourselves to a universal aspect of freedom, unifying with all that exists, then our consciousness will be able to surpass the person-based reactions and emotions. This is our hope for peace and happiness.

Whatever is related to "me" and "you" and "us" and "them" can never be totally satisfying because all of us are lacking in perfection. Our limited, contracted hearts and minds will never bring complete happiness, but the direction towards the pure and beautiful in ourselves and the world around us will provide access to transcendental consciousness. This gives us the opportunity to see that our emotions are directing all our mind states. If these remain within the narrow confines of duality and the accepted reality of our sense contacts, we cannot create the security of inner joy and peace which all of us yearn for. Most of us are not searching for a continual "high" but rather a feeling of contentment. Finding purity in our own heart means we can relate that to all around us. To the pure in heart all is pure.

The consciousness with which all of us operate differs from moment to moment, always based on our emotions. We know from our own experience that just from morning to noon our emotions have changed many times and our whole inner being changed with them. Possibly early in the morning the world looked quite pleasant, but at ten o'clock it looked terrible. Why is that? It's the same world, isn't it? But our inner life changed. To become master of our own emotions requires introspection, honesty and more attention to our feelings, and the realization that whatever creates dukkha is a defilement. Whether we have actually noticed our negativity is not important, as long as we know that dukkha is due to our own reactions.

If we could just remember that each of us is one human being in four billion on a planet which is a speck in one galaxy—the Buddha had jurisdiction over ten thousand galaxies—then we might be able to put our own desires in a somewhat better perspective. The way in which we look at ourselves and others is quite out of proportion to the immensity of all existence. When we consider also the inherent unsatisfactoriness of the infinity of all manifestations, surely that tiny bit of suffering within ourselves becomes totally insignificant. We can open ourselves up to that totality and immensity over and over again, which is possible only when the heart base does not contract with our own problems and our own reactions. We can partake in an awareness of a large, transcending reality which has no barriers. Eventually, this results in the feeling and inner knowing that within all existence there is nothing that's desirable. Ten thousand galaxies are not desirable, neither are a hundred thousand; one person isn't, neither are two or three.

If such a consciousness is brought to bear on our emotionalism there will gradually be results. Emotionalism, as opposed to emotions, is becoming affected by whatever happens, and reacting without having control. Emotions such as loving-kindness, compassion, joy with others and equanimity are the ones that purify and make it possible for the heart to become soft, pliable, luminous and expansive. Negative emotions contract the heart base, positive ones expand it. Only then can we reach out towards the universality of existence. When the heart is contracted it only sees itself. When we are very unhappy, we aren't the least bit interested in ten thousand galaxies, are we? All we want to know is how to get out of that unhappiness. That's a contracted consciousness. If we hate someone who has hurt us, we aren't concerned that there are four billion other people on this planet. Being only interested in our hate results in a contracted heart base.

When we learn to let go of these reactions, we expand our heart base which results in the expansion of our consciousness, somewhat like a stretching exercise. If done often enough, it will not shrink again. In our everyday life we have innumerable occasions to work with and check our own reactions. As we do this, we are practising Dhamma.

The heart as the seat of consciousness needs to be cared for, attended to and made much of. If we can expand it to the point where we transcend the two-dimensional way of seeing reality and have no more barriers between ourselves and the rest of the world, we will lose our personality belief. This promises the only lasting happiness.

Chapter 10

Uprooting the Wrong View of Self

Uprooting the wrong view of self means complete enlightenment. But since digging out deep roots is not an overnight affair, it stands to reason that we need to start right now. Uprooting a big tree is a tedious and difficult job and we have to use all the physical energy available. In the case of "self" we have to use all our mental energy to dig out such a deep-rooted and far-reaching root system which pervades us completely.

We can realize from our own personal experience that our wrong view of self is an enormous burden, which makes life difficult and creates constant tension. To look after this elusive "self" is an unnecessary expenditure of energy for we can hardly ever satisfy the ego's demands. We are constantly on the look-out for the right kind of person who is as attentive to us as we require. Such people do not exist because everyone cares most about themselves. This is one of the miseries of personal relationships of any kind, in families, or between student and teacher, or in communities.

Uprooting the Wrong View of Self

During the Buddha's lifetime, King Pasenadi of a neighbouring kingdom quarrelled with his wife, Queen Mallikā. He accused her of being an upstart. She had been raised by him from a low social position and was famous now and everyone was reverential to her. He said that she was only concerned with herself and although he was the cause for her wealth and position as queen, she was taking him for granted and was even feeling superior. He was so upset that he would not talk to her. When the Buddha came to visit them, he realized that the queen was not present and inquired after her. The king told the Buddha his story. The Buddha asked to have Mallikā called and explained to both of them that it was normal to think mostly about oneself.

After the Buddha left, Queen Mallikā said to her husband: "Whom do you love best? Your country, me, your children, your wealth, being king, or yourself?" He thought a while and replied honestly: "I love myself best." Then the king turned to his wife and asked her "Whom do you love best? Your children, your wealth, the people of the kingdom, me or yourself?" He was hoping she might say that she loved him most, but she also replied that she loved herself best. Again he wouldn't talk to her because he was disappointed. He went to see the Buddha and recounted their conversation. The Buddha said: "Everyone loves himself or herself best; this is the way of human nature." He also told the king to make peace with Queen Mallikā, which he did.

While we still have our "self" intact, that's the one we love best. We won't find anybody who will love us as much as we do ourselves. Yet, because of our ego delusion, we believe that there must be somebody like that somewhere. In reality we should look at this search in a different way. We shouldn't try to find somebody who will help us to support our self-delusion but rather someone who will help us to get rid of it. That can be the Buddha and his teaching, because such is the essence of the Dhamma.

Introspection shows us the difficulties in making the self solid and secure. In fact, this is such a burden that we cannot be deeply happy. We can be pleasurably excited but complete happiness is not possible with a view which needs constant reinforcement. We are not satisfied with telling ourselves how wonderful and clever we are. We need another person to reinforce and support this view.

The bigger our self-image is, the easier it gets knocked down. We often believe that it is sensitivity when our feelings are easily hurt, but it just means that we are self-centred and want to protect our threatened ego.

To look for total satisfaction for oneself is a futile endeavour. Neither satisfaction nor self really exist. Since everything changes from moment to moment, where can self and where can satisfaction be found? Yet these are the two things that the whole world is looking for and it sounds quite reasonable, doesn't it? But since these are impossible to find everybody is unhappy. Not necessarily because of tragedies, poverty, sickness or death; simply because of unfulfilled desire. Everybody is looking for something that isn't available. It is worse than looking for a needle in a haystack; at least the needle is there, even though it is hard to find. But satisfaction and self are both delusions, so how can they ever be found? Searching here and there keeps everyone busy on this little globe of ours. If we were to stop looking for satisfaction for the self, we would have an immediate lessening of dukkha, since dukkha arises only from wanting something. Also our self concept would be minimized as ego is no longer constantly in the forefront of the mind.

To get to this enormous root system which entangles us, we have to use mindfulness. The reason we find it so difficult to be really mindful is the fact that true attention shows us that there is no person, only mind and body. It is like coming up against a wall and instead of digging through that wall, the mind veers off and doesn't want to know anything further. True mindfulness has arisen when there is only the action but no doer. With divided mindfulness we experience both, the one who is mindful and the one who is being watched. If we use precision in our attention, we see—even if only for a moment—that no person is embedded in our mind/body process. We can never forget that experience.

First, letting go of the search for self satisfaction; second, mindfulness with detailed precision; and third, concentration are our means of getting at the ego root-system. There cannot be a person who is concentrated apart from the concentration, so we need to drop all thoughts and self concerns when we want to meditate properly. Then we will experience moments of nobody being there. If there is such an experience and not just a mental verbalization, it must perforce change our reactions to all that impinges on us. The more often we are able to repeat the experience, the more impact this will have on our self concept.

Our next tool can be our sense contacts, which are continuous during our waking hours. Our attention goes to the one that is the strongest. At this moment the strongest may be the thought processes. If we are just sitting, it could be the touch contact. We can fathom that the senses are being bombarded all the time and that is what we call "the world"; there isn't anything else. Even on an island in a lake with nobody around there is a lack of peacefulness through one's senses which are creating turmoil and attachments in the mind.

Attachment means we are stuck. If we are attached to sitting in the kitchen and leaning on the kitchen table, we will have to stay there until we can let go. If we are hanging on to anything at all, we can't go anywhere, can we? Intellectually we would like to be free, liberated and peaceful, but our likes and dislikes are in the way. It's like a tug-of-war within ourselves, unresolved and creating pain again and again.

Spiritual practice while hanging on to our old attachments can still bring moments of feeling peaceful and free, but it can also bring frustration. We oscillate between what we want and what we should do. Sometimes being proud and at other times guilty. None of that brings us nearer to the reality of being.

Inquiry into "who sees," "who knows," may yield some new insight into our mind's reaction to the steady stream of input through our sense doors. When we become aware of how our sense contacts are a real burden to us, then dispassion towards worldly pleasures sets in. Why do we need to burden ourselves with what we see and hear and think? At that time we are loosening the bondage of wrong view of self. When we make use of these different methods to let go of our preconceived ideas of who we are, we gradually see a different underlying reality. The world is our sense contacts which generate craving for pleasure and comfort. Is that worthwhile pursuing or is it better dropped? That's a decision we make with head and heart when we realize that restlessness ensues from our senses which are continually reaching for satisfaction. Because there is no total satisfaction and also no self to be found, we are going in the wrong direction. However, we can live in stillness and peace when we get rid of our habitual striving and start at the other end. We can watch with precise attention, knowing all sense contacts for what they are, drop our search for happiness, inquire into our reactions, and concentrate in meditation. All these steps combined will get us to the roots of our being, so we can start digging them out.

When we change the way we look at ourselves, everything else falls into place. A completely different picture emerges like a kaleidoscope which has been turned around. This is an experiment worth trying.

Chapter 11

Twelve Conditions Leading to Nibbāna

The Mahā Assapura Sutta (Majjhima Nikāya 29) outlines an exact course of action which leads to Nibbāna. Each step on the way brings more ease, more understanding and the ability to see more clearly. Not knowing what is *really* important and what is not is caused by the obstructions in heart and mind. The more obstructions there are, and the less mind-training there is, the heavier is the accumulation. The practice, the training, is the only way out.

The course of action that the Buddha recommends begins with conscience and shame (*hiriottappa*)—the guardians of the world. Without these guardians the world and humanity as we know them would fall apart. If we were not ashamed to misbehave, if we were not afraid of being censured by our fellow men, if we were not afraid of being punished, then chaos would prevail. We would live in anarchy. The fact that all societies need police shows that shame and fear are not always operating. For instance, the atrocities committed in Germany under Hitler were the result of the lack of shame and fear.

When shame and fear are absent, we see the breakdown of human relationships. When shame and fear do not come forth as "guardians", negative emotions prevail. If we were not subject to hate, disgust, rejection, resistance, worry, fear, jealousy and pride, then there could never be a breakdown of human interactions. We would always be ashamed of anything inside of us that was not totally pure. Our conscience and the fear of wrong-doing would always operate, at all levels and at all times.

All of us do have a conscience. But do we always heed its warning?

Jiminy Cricket used to sing: "Always let your conscience be your guide." This is sound advice which we need to follow. We must not allow this guide to be over-shadowed and overridden by desire, for that is when relationships deteriorate and our own personal life becomes difficult. Hazards arise whenever our inner voice has been silenced in favour of trying to get something—be it recognition, praise, acceptance, being right, or even good meditation.

The whole course of action that the Buddha proclaims is based on introspection. Mindfulness needs to be constant, not an on-and-off affair. How else can we keep in touch with our conscience? How else can we know if there is anything to be ashamed of?

The Buddha said: "One should be so afraid of breaking a precept, of doing something wrong, as if one is already standing with one foot in hell."

This is the fear that keeps us on the Noble Path; the fear of doing something wrong.

Purification of bodily, verbal and mental conduct is the next three steps. If we haven't done any purification in one of these three modes each day, then we have wasted that day. What a pity! That day can never be recaptured, it's gone forever. We can use every single day for something valuable—if we are living with awareness. The Buddha describes this step as being frank, totally truthful and open about ourselves. We can see ourselves as we really are.

Being totally aware also helps us to refrain from automatic responses and mechanical instinctive behaviour. Far too often our habits, since we are so often unmindful, lead us into unwholesomeness through body, speech and thoughts. Our training means no longer reacting to get more and have more for ourselves. We investigate instead what we say, what we think, what we do. We find out whether we are rendering a service and if we are truly loving and considerate. If we are not, then we can quickly change our course of action. As we investigate these three doors: thought, speech and action, and purify and restrain them, we not only come to know the truth about ourselves, but we have the opportunity of connecting with others in the Dhamma way.

Right livelihood is the fourth purification. We must take care of our necessities; not by taking from others, not by asking to be given, but by offering our skills and our time. At one level, livelihood can be considered just as a way to make money, but what is really meant is earning one's livelihood as a part of the spiritual life.

The right kind of livelihood which is purified, restrained, frank and open, is one in which generosity has topmost priority. The opposite of generosity is grasping, keeping it all for ourselves. And that means ego-centredness.

In relative truth, we think we need to keep something for a rainy day. If we don't look after ourselves, how can we feel secure? However, in absolute truth there is no "my self" to be looked after. The ordinary person with a mundane way of thinking cannot operate on both levels. It's like having two railroad tracks: if we're travelling on one, we can't be on the other. We have to have a switch in order to connect with a different train. Through experience, through purification and refinement, both "tracks" can be discerned.

The next step in the course of purification leading to Nibbāna is the restraint and the guarding of the sense faculties. "Right worthy of gifts is the Sangha purified, with pacified senses, all mental stains removed." How do we guard the senses? The Buddha says: "Guarding the senses so that no signs of formations arise which make evil, unprofitable dhammas arise in one." This means that when we see something beautiful, we do not covet it. As soon as we want what we see, we've lost that round. Or we may hear something that is not in accord with what we are thinking, and we have a hate reaction. Well, another round lost.

Guarding our senses means guarding our mind. Not letting the mind think anything it pleases and run wild. Guarding the mind, so that it only thinks that which is profitable, helpful and pure. The mind must come to the point that, when it is thinking something which is not totally pure, there is such an unpleasant feeling that we quickly drop it, as if we were burning ourselves. That unpleasant feeling has to be our guide. Unless there is a feeling of total equanimity, a total feeling of peace, of being at ease and loving, there is something wrong with the thinking process. There has arisen either greed (wanting) or hate (dislike).

It is very easy to see these in ourselves if we are awake, really awake. If we rationalize: "Yes, but in this case I can't do it," or "In this case it's useless," or "In this case it's necessary," even though it sounds believable, the feeling inside does not become any better. Only when we are feeling really at ease and at peace has the mind acted in the proper way. We have to watch and guard the mind when seeing, hearing, tasting, touching, smelling. Guarding means not letting the mind run after pleasant sensations, not letting the mind run towards disliking the unpleasant situations, just letting them all be.

The world is full of pleasant and unpleasant sensations. We can't have all the pleasant ones; we can't resist and dislike all the unpleasant ones; nor are we going to change the world. Nothing out there is going to change. Everything is going to keep on going exactly the same way it always has. Namely, from pleasant to unpleasant and back to unpleasant. Up and down, back and forth, a constant seesaw effect. At times we're up and then we're down. Unless we guard our sense faculties, we'll keep on blaming the objects of our sense consciousness, that which our senses contact. We'll keep on blaming the outer conditions which trigger reactions in us. Let's make a sign and hang it up over our beds: "Don't blame the trigger." Unless we start doing that, well, there's no end. We must start somewhere. Unless we get a grip on ourselves, there is no spiritual life. There's no use sitting in meditation if we don't start doing something about our heart and mind.

Don't blame the trigger! There isn't anything to blame, it's all happening inside. Shame, conscience, verbal, mental and bodily action, sense faculties, have nothing to do with anybody or anything. They have to do with where we are, whether we meditate or not. They have nothing to do with whom we talk to, whom we live with, what we know, what's happening in the world. They have to do with ourselves. Unless we get started with that, there is no Noble Path.

When we react, all that is happening is that the sense contacts are triggering us to react. It's interesting, this reaction machine. In fact, it is fascinating. Somebody says something we like: wow, it feels nice. Then somebody says something we don't like, bingo, the whole thing starts. There it goes again—down. We think it's the other person. However, it's never really the other one, it has nothing to do with anyone else. The world has four billion people. They don't care how we react. Only we care how we react. We're the only one who cares, the only one it means anything to. This means being frank and open to ourselves. This is introspection. Unless there is truth within ourselves, the path to liberation, to Nibbāna, is not open.

Guarding the senses means the minimization of desires. We don't want so much. And what we don't have doesn't matter so much because the senses are not connecting all the time. If we walk along the street and it's full of shop windows which are displaying the most wonderful merchandise, and the eye connects to all these things, then obviously the mind's going to say, "Hey, that would come in very handy, that looks good, it's cheap, I think I'll get one of those." If we don't walk down that street, we don't even see the shops. If we don't know what they have for sale, then the mind doesn't say a thing. Guarding the senses means seeing all that stuff and still not connecting.

The next step after guarding the sense faculties is moderation in eating. Moderation in eating is mentioned by the Buddha as an antidote for two of our hindrances: for sensual desire, and for sloth and torpor. It doesn't mean not to eat anything, but just to eat in moderation, knowing exactly what we need and not having any more than that. Eating is one desire which all living beings have and can, in most cases, be easily satisfied. Food is available. And if we don't let ourselves go, then we have already learned to guard one of the sense faculties.

The next step on this path is mindfulness, mindfulness at all times. First the Buddha mentions wakefulness and connects it to mindfulness. In this particular discourse he talks about sleeping two hours a night. Certainly not at times when it is ill-advised, but when conditions are right. Two hours sleep a night and being totally mindful the rest of the time. Mindful and fully aware the whole day. If we were to do that, the Buddha said, completely, utterly and perfectly, we could become enlightened in just seven days. He was speaking of total mindfulness, but even a little bit will go a long way. Mindful and fully aware is the only way we can get in touch with what's going on inside of us. If we don't have mindfulness, we won't be able to hear our own conscience. If we don't have mindfulness, we won't be able to guard our sense faculties.

Mindfulness is the only mental factor we have which makes it possible for us to understand what is happening inside of us. Without that we are not practising, and not training ourselves: If we are not training ourselves we are going to be the same as we've always been. If we were satisfied with the way we have always been, we wouldn't be sitting in meditation and listening to the Dhamma. So it's a foregone conclusion that we are not satisfied. It is advisable not to be satisfied with the way we are, because that is complacency.

Complacency is one of the greatest hindrances for all affluent societies. Complacent people are the type who will say, "I don't need this meditation. I am perfectly happy. You must be very unhappy if you want to meditate. Whatever I've done is O.K." This is a kind of unaware, unawake state, which has no mindfulness in it at all. To practise mindfulness means that we have the ability to get to know what's going on inside of ourselves. We've awakened to ourselves. If we don't wake up to ourselves, who are we going to wake up to? Does it really matter whether someone else can meditate? Does it really matter whether someone else is happy? Does it really matter whether someone else is going to be enlightened? Or does it matter whether we can meditate? Does it matter whether we're happy, whether we're on the right path?

Becoming aware and awake to ourselves. Everything else is just another movie. Instead of being able to go to a movie, or turn on the television, we just make up our own movies, that's all. As many as possible. They're not even very entertaining. They're usually depressing. They have a momentary feeling about them that doesn't last very long.

This mindfulness and full awareness which the Buddha talks about is strictly concerned with daily living. He hasn't even got around to meditation yet, in the sequence of this discourse. Meditation is yet to come. All these steps mentioned are concerned with our ordinary day to day activities, moment to moment living. Meditation will be coming, and certainly it is absolutely essential, but these activities have to precede it. Meditation will not succeed unless these activities happen first.

The full awareness of ourselves, connected to mindfulness, makes it possible to see inside of ourselves—to see the hindrances, the obstructions, the defilements. And what is the course of action to get from here to there? It's one of the most useful and fascinating aspects of the Buddha's teachings that he gives us an exact explanation of how to get from where we are to where we could be. It's a road map, but we can't be armchair travellers. There are so many of those in the world. People sit at home and read maps instead of going on trips. That same thing is done with the Buddha's teachings. The maps are there and they are very exact and there are landmarks given so we can see where we are and know the next step.

After having established mindfulness in daily living, we sit down with legs crossed, with body erect and mindfulness established before us. We don't talk about the states of absorption here, or watching the breath, rather becoming mindful and totally attentive to our hindrances in the meditation process. This is an interesting aspect as quite often the Buddha talks about becoming aware of the hindrances in meditation, using that as a meditation subject.

The Buddha speaks of establishing mindfulness so that one realizes what is arising which is not skilful, not wholesome, not beneficial. He speaks of labelling, which I have so often advocated. Know what is arising, give it a name. Know what it is. Unless we know what it is, how are we going to change it? Giving it a name also makes it more accessible. Imagine a person around here whose name we do not know. It would be difficult to have an intimate acquaintance with that person. The person is not really accessible to us. In not knowing the name, we do not know who the person is. It's a stranger. However, when we can at least put a name on what we are connected with—a person or a defilement—it becomes an acquaintance, no longer a stranger. Our defilements should be at least our acquaintances. If they're not, how are we going to do anything about them? So we must give them a name.

There are five hindrances which comprise the main heading of everything that is wrong with us and also all other human beings. This is never just a personal difficulty, it is universal. Unless we see that universality of it all, it is always going to be heavy. Either it's "poor little me," or "bad little me," or it's "wonderful little me" or "wonderful great me, I'm not as bad as you are," or "I'm worse than you are"—all of that ego talk. What we need to do is not talk about or think about ourselves in any of these ways, but label what is actually arising, that which is coming up, and if nothing is coming up, it means we're asleep. I don't mean necessarily physically asleep. I mean that we're mentally asleep, we don't know what is coming up; the awareness hasn't started.

The five hindrances are sensual desire, ill-will, sloth and torpor, restlessness and worry, and sceptical doubt. All five are like huge granite blocks sitting in the heart and mind and obstructing the path. The path to where? Well, mainly the path to happiness. They're blocking the way and making it impossible to get by. They're holding us up and we can't shift them. They're much too heavy. What we have to learn is to see them for what they are and replace them.

There are antidotes which the Buddha has prescribed. The one which is the same for all five is "noble friends and noble conversation." In ourselves we are not capable enough. If we were, why, we'd be enlightened. In America it is said, "If you're so smart why aren't you rich?" If we can do it ourselves, why haven't we done it? What's stopping us? Our blindness is stopping us.

The noble friends and the noble conversation are what can help us on this path. Without having some help somewhere along the line, it is very rare that a person can make it. There was such a person and that was the Buddha. He did it on his own. He went to teachers to learn meditation, but he did not learn from them how to get rid of the unsatisfactoriness (dukkha). He found it himself. There are occasional sages who can find the way by themselves, but it is highly unlikely that we are one of them.

Noble friends are those who point to our mistakes rather than commiserating with our difficulties and saying how badly the world has treated us. The world treats everybody badly who reacts to it badly. A person who is a noble friend would be a person who would help us to see what is really happening inside of us. A noble conversation would be a conversation about the Dhamma, about that which is true. The word Dhamma means the Buddha's teachings, it means the law of nature, and it means truth.

The antidote of noble friends and noble conversation is the antidote for all five hindrances. Sloth and torpor means not having energy, especially when it counts. At night, when it's time to go to sleep, it's obviously alright to go to sleep. But in the day time it's a different story. The Buddha compares that with being in prison. Nobody likes to be in prison—imprisoned by one's own lack of energy. When we have sensual desires, when the world is beckoning with its manifold enticements: that can all be called one thing only, namely Māra, the tempter. If we can then be reminded of the truth of the Dhamma, we can again and again find our footing. If we can't be reminded, it's highly unlikely that we're going to remind ourselves. It's too easy to fall into Māra's trap. Māra never lets up; temptation never lets up until the moment of enlightenment. The Buddha was being tempted while sitting under the Bodhi tree, moments before becoming enlightened. If that happened to him, what about us?

Our situation is one in which temptation is constant. It doesn't necessarily have to be that we want to go travelling, go swimming, go surfing, go water-skiing or whatever may attract us. Maybe we just want to chatter. Idle chatter is one of the aspects of the fourth precept, "right speech." Idle chatter is considered to be wrong speech. It's one aspect of wrong speech and the world with its glitter tempts us to do that. Noble conversation is the Dhamma.

There are temptations everywhere and if we see them as such, then we can do something about them. If we don't see them as such, then of course there is nothing we can do. There is no blame attached to any of that, it's the recognition which counts. When we have sensual desires, they aren't always so easily understood. They don't necessarily have to be that we want a chocolate malt. Maybe we don't even like chocolate malt, or sailing a boat. But these sensual desires go in many other directions and we have to watch and be aware that each of our desires anchors us to dukkha like a hook that hooks us. Even when we get the gratification, even then it's dukkha, because the gratification can't last. It's momentary.

All that watching can be done in the meditation process when we sit down and establish the mindfulness process. When the Buddha uses these words, he means that we are fully aware of the defilements and are able to let them go in order to really start meditation. Following the thinking process during meditation is sensual desire. It's more pleasant and entertaining to let the mind wander than to put in real effort to gain concentration. It's not only entertaining, it's ego confirming. As long as one is thinking, one at least knows that the ego exists in full force. And as long as one is thinking, one nurtures that ego. When one no longer thinks, there can come the moment of losing the "I" identification. And in the first instance that can be a scary moment.

Ill-will is easily seen in the meditation process. Maybe it's ill-will towards one's bodily discomforts. Maybe it's ill-will towards something someone else has said or done. Maybe it's ill-will against a group of people, or a situation in the world. It doesn't matter what kind of ill-will it is—ill-will is ill-will. It is hate. It is dislike, distrust. And although it is very unpleasant in our heart, fortunately it is so unpleasant that it is the easiest of the defilements to get rid of. We realize its detrimental effects.

Sensual desire, which is greed, always promises something nice to happen, some sensual gratification. Therefore it doesn't feel unpleasant, it feels exciting. Am I going to get it? Will I be able to keep it? That feeling of hope and expectation is not unpleasant at all and therefore extremely difficult to eradicate. It's not only difficult to get rid of, it's also difficult to notice. Most people in the world who haven't practised meditation don't even know they have desire for sense gratification. Practically everything they do is triggered by sensual desire, whatever it may be. Only those who practise and establish mindfulness before them in the meditative process can become aware of this constant wish for pleasant sensation, whether it be physical or emotional: "I'd like to have it nice. I'd like to hear only that which sounds nice to me, feel only the things that feel good."

It is extremely difficult to get rid of the first hindrance of sensual desire because it seems so natural. The response often is, and I've heard it several times: "Well, what's wrong with that? Surely I don't want unpleasant sensation, do I?" No, surely not. But the wanting is the dukkha and the wanting is the hook. It's the hook on which we get caught. The ill-will, the anger, the hate are very unpleasant, feel awful, and therefore are easier to get rid of. If we realize the anger, the hatred and the ill-will inside of ourselves we will take

94

definite steps to get rid of them, if shown how to do it, and if realizing that we are making no one else unhappy except ourselves. And that's not very hard to see. It is easier to live with a greedy person.

But it is more difficult for that person to let go of greed. Such a person likes what she has, and what she wants. The hate character is much more difficult to have around, but it is easier to work with hate. No one likes hate in himself, so it is more easily renounced. There was a great meditation master in Thailand who used to say: "I only want such disciples who are hate characters. They're much easier to teach. They get the idea almost immediately." Now, obviously anybody who has hate, also has greed and anybody who has greed, also has hate. These are only mentioned in this context as to which is predominant in a person.

In meditation itself, when we are aware and awake to ourselves and label, we know what is arising. We can see it. If I really want those pleasant sensations to arise over and over again, then obviously that's greed. If I dislike my sitting position and it isn't comfortable to sit like that, and I don't like the person talking, well, obviously that's hate. It's very easy to see that when we are true to ourselves, honest with ourselves. And if we aren't honest with ourselves, there's no one else with whom to be honest. The only person who counts is oneself. Everything else is society, which doesn't count on the spiritual path. Honesty towards and about ourselves is one of the ten virtues, truth (*sacca*).

Restlessness and worry is past and future. When it arises in the thinking process in meditation, we can see quite clearly that we worry about the future. Am I going to have enough money? Am I going to keep my health? Am I going to be able to organize my affairs in a way that will be pleasing? Worry about the future is absurd, to say the least, because that future may never happen. When we think money is needed or whatever we think we need, this is totally imaginary; we may not be alive to live this future. Secondly, the person who experiences that future isn't the person who is worrying about it. It's an entirely different person. The person who is worrying is not going to have the result of that worry. So we might as well drop it, forget it. We are a different person from second to second.

Restlessness has its roots in the past, in most cases in having something left undone. There arises a feeling of "I've got to do it now, or it may be too late," of "Life is going by me". The fear that we are missing out on something may happen in meditation. We sit trying to get organized, concentrated, and the mind starts throwing up all sorts of ideas of what we could be doing instead. Well, there's no end to what we could be doing instead, absolutely no end to that list. I can't even start giving that list because I would never finish it. The mind doesn't finish with it either. The things that we think of very often are those things we aren't done with yet. It is Māra talking again. Restlessness arises from that, because we think that really the one thing that we haven't tried yet, will answer our problems.

Both of these, restlessness and worry are energy drains. They take away energy that we need for meditation. If we use our energy for those two, we are cheating ourselves. Restlessness and worry are useless; they don't produce anything. And yet they take away from us the ability to really see clearly. It is as if we are drowning. We can drown in worry, we can drown in restlessness. These then throw up a lot of thoughts, and unless they are labelled and named, we can't get at them.

Fear is not specifically mentioned. Fear has the aspect of hate and ill-will. And fear also has the aspect of worry and restlessness. Fear of other people is a lack of love. Fear of the future is the lack of self-confidence. Fear of not being able to handle something, or the fear of not getting what we want is connected with sensual desire. There is the fear of not having pleasant sensations because we lack expertise. There are so many fears and they are always based on the fear that the ego will not be supported.

What about our good friend, sceptical doubt? Sceptical doubt is traditionally explained in this way. Was the Buddha really enlightened? Is the Dhamma really the truth? Does the Sangha really know what they are talking about? This sceptical doubt stops us from practice. The Buddha often speaks about hearing the truth and then acting upon it. If we're sceptical, then whatever we hear we try to compare with what we already know. What we know is not on the same level as absolute truth. There's no comparison. We can't compare it, no matter how we try. So we are blocked. That which we hear isn't doing us any good, nor that which we already know. We are sitting between two chairs.

That which we hear which is concerned with Dhamma is totally different from anything else. The same words, the same language, the same kind of ideas mean something entirely different. That which we know is questionable in any case. A comparison between the two cannot be made. There's no connection. Sceptical doubt tries to make a connection.

Sceptical doubt also concerns our own lack of ability. Are we really going to be able to meditate, to continue a spiritual path, really be able to let go? All this is a lack of self-confidence. That kind of doubt in oneself can be overcome if one sees one can do something more than what was previously done. We can sit through a meditation session, we can actually concentrate the mind, we can let go of ill-will. It is our own action which gives us confidence.

But sceptical doubt in the teaching must eventually be overcome because the teaching leads to

Nibbāna and Nibbāna cannot be experienced if there is any doubt. One has to have confidence in something unknown. This is the case in many instances. We learn to swim. It's totally unknown to us whether we can swim or not. Lots of little kids scream their heads off in fear. A lot don't. They have a bit of confidence that the teacher who is teaching them knows what she is talking about and they just go in the water and try. They don't know whether it's going to work. Those are the ones who learn to swim. The ones who are standing on the shore, screaming their heads off, have to go home again. They are not going to learn to swim. That bit of confidence has to be there to try that which is unknown, and see whether one can actually do it. Unless one gives oneself that chance, one is never going to discover whether anything works. This means emptying oneself of one's own ideas. How we think it is, how it should be done, how the truth actually is, what the spiritual life is all about, how it should he lived, what people in the spiritual life should be doing, how they should look and talk, how we should look and talk— these are all ideas which create roadblocks to experiencing something new.

People have all sorts of ideas about what nuns or monks should be doing with themselves from morning till night, or how they should conduct themselves, or how one should approach them; all are personal ideas. If these ideas are strong enough and the reality isn't in accord with them, the whole practice collapses. Why? Because it is not in accord with our own ideas. Yet the world is not in accord with our ideas. It's not doing what we think it should. It also doesn't look as we think it should. This is a thinking-process which one day has to be dropped.

Nibbāna is emptiness. Emptiness of what? We have read the Shorter Discourse on Emptiness (Majjhima Nikāya 121) about that—emptiness of villages, emptiness of forests, emptiness of this and that and eventually emptiness of all formations. Why not get a glimpse of that emptiness? Chuck out the whole rigmarole that's going on in the mind. Chuck it out and see what it's like then. It's free, it's easy, it's joyful, there's nothing in it, no great big granite blocks of desire and hate, sloth and torpor, restlessness, worry or doubt, nothing in it, empty.

An empty mind is not a vegetable mind. An empty mind is empty of its own ideation. An empty mind is empty of mental formations. When the seeing is only seeing, the hearing is only hearing, and the cognizing is only cognizing, the mind doesn't answer. That's when enlightenment is possible There can be glimpses of that. Nibbāna is not eons away. Nibbāna is only the five hindrances away. Naming them, knowing them, gets us one step nearer to freedom. The defilements become old acquaintances. And once in a while when one of them has become an old acquaintance, we can greet it with: "Ah, are you back again? Haven't I told you many times to stay away?" Then you give a little smile about your-self and think: "Well, there it is again. And I thought I had that one taken care of. And now it's come back."

These are old acquaintances that we are trying to work with. Becoming so well acquainted with them that we know exactly how to handle them. Just like the people we know really well. We know how to handle them. When they get all upset we know what to do. Some of them we want to walk away from; they want to be left alone. Others we just want to sit with and listen to their miseries. Others might like to get a little sympathy. Some we might humour. We just know how to handle them, because they're old acquaintances. These defilements must become old acquaintances. When they appear, we know what to do with them. Every so often we can give them a smile and say: "I do know you very well, but I'd thought you'd gone away for a while." Having done that in meditation, in this particular sequence of events that the Buddha describes, there comes the moment of the hindrances not arising in the meditation. It doesn't mean that they have been uprooted. They get uprooted at total enlighten-ment, total liberation, total insight. But they don't arise at that time because they have been recog-nised for what they are and have been let go of in meditation. That's when it is possible to go into the meditative absorptions (*jhānas*).

Whenever the Buddha talks about concentration, *samādhi* meditation, he is talking about states of absorption (jhānas). The Buddha does not go into great detail about them. He gives some particulars, but it's not possible to give much explanation about mental states that are utterly different from the ones we are usually acquainted with. Our language does not suffice; it is concerned with daily activities. The jhānas are certainly not everyday activities. There are not so many people who are able to go into the jhānas, so there isn't a great deal of language about it. The words the Buddha uses are the ordinary everyday words we use for everything else, so they cannot possibly give an exact description, only an approximate one. The Buddha says about the first jhāna that one has "initial application and continued application," which means we first sit down and get concentrated and apply ourselves to the concentration. And then we are able to keep it going. From that arises "physical rapture, bodily pleasant feeling" (*pīti*). *Pīti* may be very strong at times, and sometimes not so strong. It depends on the concentration. That is the extent of the first jhāna. There is, of course, one-pointed attention to that.

The second jhana is the one which creates self-confidence because it doesn't need initial and continued application; we just do it. Having been able to be immersed in the first one, the second one follows. We don't need to initially apply ourselves, or continue to apply ourselves. The concentration has come to the point where it is not necessary to start all over again. In the beginning, when we start with the jhānas, pleasant physical feelings arise and in order to continue one has to apply the mind with determination. When the second jhāna has been established there's no such need. Because of that the mind becomes confident that it is able to do what it wants to do.

An ordinary mind is always feeling attacked by outer conditions, by other people, by one's own discomforts, by one's own ideas: it gets thrown about in many directions. It cannot rely on its own reactions. It is unsure of itself, because if something really awful were to happen, it would react accordingly. Feeling badly one might speak nastily. But a mind that is able to go into the second jhāna has the confidence to know that it can look after itself under any circumstances which will arise. In the second jhāna there is no initial or continued application, but due to the pleasant physical feeling, happiness arises. The pleasant physical feeling does not disappear, rather it fades into the background, it is no longer the predominant feature, but happiness is now one's main experience. To be really in the jhānas means one can stay concentrated in these states for the length of time one wants. One can decide how long one wishes to remain in absorption and can do so. This is the confidence creating aspect.

In the third jhāna, the pleasant physical feeling is still there, happiness is still there, but they are in the background; and a feeling of contentedness—equanimity—arises. This contentedness brings peace. One is content. One has what one wants. There is nothing which one desires. One has the state of mind that is satisfying.

In the fourth jhāna, the pleasant physical feeling and the happiness go away, and the only thing which remains is the equanimity, with absolute and utterly pure mindfulness. Mindfulness being pure means that it has only even-mindedness as its focus. It no longer has a feeling of happiness, or peace or pleasant feeling to attend to. It is comparatively easy to stay focused on happiness and pleasant feeling because they provide a tangible meditation subject. To stay focused on equanimity is more difficult as one's awareness has to be very bright and finely tuned. The fourth jhāna is a more refined state and moments of it have to be cultivated in order to sustain it for the length of time one has decided upon.

The Buddha mentions many times that the jhānas are pleasant abidings. They are not the goal, but they are the pathway to the goal. Many meditation masters say that a little bit of insight creates a little bit of calm, and a little bit of calm creates a little bit of insight. If there isn't any meditative calm, neither pleasant feelings nor happiness arise.

Continue working on insight, which means naming whatever arises in ourselves. Know what it is and see it for what it is, having its own origination, its cause for arising, having its own deterioration. Whatever arises has to cease. See the danger in it and see the escape from it. How has it arisen? How is it ceasing? Why is it dangerous? Now, I can escape from it by letting go. These are moments of insight which will create calm, and calm creates insight.

The mind which is totally calm, which is not bothered by anything, not by hate nor greed, can see the world and self differently. We cannot go into the jhānas if there is hate or greed. First we must see the hindrances and drop them momentarily, so that the jhānas can be established. The mind that can do that and is in a state of total seclusion from the hindrances is a mind which can have an entirely different inner vision. It does not have the discoloration of ego at that time. When the discoloration is not there, there's a different truth. This different truth can only be accepted by a mind which is calm and joyful. A troubled or distracted mind cannot accept that truth because it looks too much like annihilation of the self. But it isn't that at all.

It's a letting go of delusion of self. But the mind that has not been able to attain its own inner joy cannot accept that "there's nobody there." The mind that has calm and joy will rejoice in that kind of truth because it takes the burden off one's back. The burden is gone. If there's nobody there who's having problems, who can possibly worry or fear?

Only if self has been seen for what it is, namely, a creation of craving, will the mind become so "malleable, wieldy, steady and imperturbable" that it can encompass all existence. It will then attain to a super mind-state where past and future merge into the present, where what is far merges into that which is near and where total purity and total wisdom eliminate craving and becoming. Then the holy life has been lived to perfection.

Chapter 12

The Meditative Absorptions

When we read about meditative absorption
(*jhāna*) in the Buddha's discourses, some of the
wording is unusual and creates the impression
of super-natural achievements. It may be useful
to investigate this in a little more detail.

Whatever method of meditation we use can be
termed a key. After having paid undivided attention to this key for some time, we have an intimate
understanding and knowledge of it. Then we are
able to find the keyhole, fit the key into it and
unlock the door. Having done that, we no longer
need the key, since the door is now open. We may
now dispense with the method and enter into the
inner chambers of beauty, peacefulness and
unsullied purity of our own mind, where we are
able to experience a different kind of reality.

It is, therefore, immaterial which method of
meditation we practise, as long as it will be a
useful key. However, the breath has been the
traditional and much favoured subject from the days
of old until now. Breath and mind are intrinsically
connected. When the mind becomes quiet and
tranquil, the breath follows suit. When the breath
becomes calm, it also becomes so fine and subtle
that it is difficult to find. Meditators are sometimes
afraid at this point that they are losing their breath

and with it their life-force and begin to breathe forcefully. There is no need for fear; as long as there is life, there is breath. As the breath becomes shallow and quiet, a pleasant physical feeling arises.

Although pleasant physical feelings are known to us in our everyday life, they are always connected with an outer source, which has reached us through the senses. Unless we are meditating, we would never imagine that a much more pleasant feeling in the body is possible than anything we have known in the world. This feeling is not dependent on outer conditions, but only on the inner condition of concentration. The feeling may be different for different people and may also arise in a changed form at various meditation sessions. In any case, it will always be far more pleasant than anything we have known until then. Since this is the strongest experience in our mind now, it becomes our meditation subject and we learn to keep it in mind for a solid period of time. At first it will appear only as a flash, but as we become more practised, we can stay with it for as long as we wish.

Why should it be important to experience a blissful physical feeling in meditation and what can we learn from it?

First of all, the Buddha said that in order to meditate successfully, we need to be comfortable in body and mind. Secondly, the impermanence of this most pleasant feeling will show us how fleeting all our pleasures are and will eventually make us dispassionate towards the gratification of the senses, which are keeping us bound in the realm of birth and death. Furthermore, our meditative absorptions act as a purifying method for our defilements. While we are pleasantly absorbed in blissful feelings we have no negativities in our mind, so that the mind carries less darkness around with it, as we practise steadily. Also during our daily lives, we realize that the difficulties which all of us encounter can be considered minor irritations and not major tragedies, since we have a trained mind now which is able to reach a blissful feeling on demand.

Possibly most important of all, the reason for the necessity to achieve meditative absorption is the fact that only a mind which is well trained to concentrate steadily is strong and powerful enough to penetrate the illusion in which we live and see the absolute reality which underlies it.

Having come thus far with the meditation, it is now necessary to recapitulate what has gone on, since we sat down on the pillow. Unless we find our own pathway to reach absorption, it will remain a "hit or miss" affair, which will leave us frustrated and unsatisfied. Many details may contribute towards our ability to concentrate well and we should be able to find the most important ones, so that we may repeat them time and time again, whenever we meditate.

Physically it may depend on not being too full, sitting in a comfortable posture, and with the noise outside kept at a minimum. Mentally it may depend on the input we have had prior to the meditation, that is why it is imperative to protect the jewel of our mind from being scratched or dirtied through idle chatter, gossip or tales of violence. Emotionally it may depend on starting the meditation with the practice of loving-kindness towards ourselves, our teachers, our loved ones, our companions, or starting with devotion and gratitude towards the Buddha and his teaching.

Any or all of these possibilities need to be taken into account and those that we find helpful should be used, or any others we ourselves may have experienced. Having found our pathway, we no longer lose our way in the dark and convoluted recesses of our mind, but are able to go straight towards the different stages of absorption, which are a great treasure to own. As all our minds are of the same fabric, only differentiated through our various kammas, it is easy to see that each mind will travel along the same pathway towards more expansiveness and purity. Our only individual contribution will be the details necessary for us to reach the doorway where we can turn the key and enter into the illuminated chambers of our mind. From then on our minds will all have identical experiences.

But how we understand and evaluate these experiences will again be our own responsibility;

and how much wisdom we gain from them is entirely up to our discrimination and discernment. For instance, if we regret the impermanence of the blissful feeling, we have not related to impermanence as a reality, but only as an unfortunate occurrence, which we would prefer to forget. That is not wisdom, but the reaction of a worldling, and in that case meditative absorption may not result in insight. Calm and tranquillity are the necessary and skillful means for intuitive wisdom to arise, which shows us the world as a phenomenon without substantial significance. Only then can we leave it behind without regrets or displeasure.

When we are practised in reverting to the first stage or meditative absorption, the experience of a blissful bodily feeling, we become aware of the fact that this is still a gross attainment, since it hinges on the body, with which we may no longer identify or at least not hold it in such high esteem as formerly. It is at that time that we are able to let the physical feeling go into the background of our attention and focus primarily on our emotional feeling, which must be joy and happiness at that time. Having experienced a blissful physical feeling, the emotional reaction can be no other than joyful. This then becomes our main subject of attention, while the physical bliss remains with us, but more subdued and in the background.

As we practise steadily we will be able to stay with this joyful feeling as long as we wish.

Having attained this stage in our meditation, we gain a great deal of self-confidence, because we know from our own experience that our happiness no longer depends on other people, situations, acclaim, fame, love or appreciation. It depends strictly on our meditation practice. This certainly gives us a feeling of independence and security, not to be found in worldly matters anywhere. We can say that we have found a home for our mind, where we can go for shelter any time and be protected. This will naturally colour our outlook upon the world and its temptations, as well as our vision of ourselves as part of this mundane existence. We may no longer find much to delight us in real world existence, when we can so clearly experience that no matter how luminous and exalted our mind may feel during meditation, it comes back to its confused and reactive state soon afterwards.

The difficulty which all meditators encounter is discursive thinking. Even when absorbed states have already been experienced, the mind still likes to play its games. Ego affirmation is only possible when we are thinking, and that is the indulgence which we allow ourselves when we do not discipline the mind enough to remain concentrated. Everyone has to deal with the balance between indulgence and self-discipline. The Buddha called it the Middle Path and we need individual application to ensure we do not go overboard on either side.

Having now been able to experience joy in meditation, we know it to be more subtle and refined than any state of happiness ever experienced in daily living. Yet, we also sense that it is still not as fine and super-mundane as possible and we let go of the joyful feeling to experience contentment. This appears as a less excited, more peaceful mind state, with an absence of desire, creating for the first time a feeling within which everyone craves, but none but the meditator achieves.

We can learn now that only the absence of all wishes brings contentment, and not as we may have thought until then, the fulfilment of our wishes. This is one of the most profound lessons we can learn, and while it sounds very simple, it contains the essence of the truth of suffering and its elimination.

An apt simile of these progressive states of meditative absorptions is the following: a person has been wandering through the desert without any water and is parched and searches for relief. Finally the person's eyes alight on a pond of water in the distance. The mind registers pleasurable excitement that relief is so near. This describes the first stage of meditative absorption, when pleasant feelings arise and a sense of excitement is experienced.

Then the parched and thirsty person draws near to the water pond and stands quite close to it. Happiness ensues that the elimination of suffering is now on hand, and the mind is suffused with a buoyant joyous feeling. This explains the second stage of absorption when the pleasurable physical feeling goes into the background and joy comes into the foreground, but excitement has not yet abated, only lessened.

Now, the thirsty person drinks the water and experiences the anticipated relief and feels contented in having gained the desired objective, namely water for quenching the thirst. This explains the third stage of absorption, when the mind, having gained the objective of joy, now feels contented and loses its desires.

Having drunk enough, the no-longer-thirsty person lies down in the shade under a tree and experiences the peace of fulfilment. This describes the fourth stage of meditative absorption which goes into deeper recesses of the mind where total peacefulness can be felt, since all desires are fulfilled and no mental action needs to be taken.

This fourth stage of absorption is the most refined meditation state in the fine-material realm. It is called so because all four aspects of these absorptions are known to us in the material realm, but are much more refined and satisfying when they arise through concentration. Not only are we familiar with pleasant physical feelings, joy and contentment, but we also know peace, yet what we know outside of meditation cannot be compared in quality to what we can experience with a pure and luminous mind in meditation. Quite apart from the fact that we are no longer dependent on outer factors to make us feel peaceful, we are now able to enter into the depth of this whenever we wish.

To gain access to this fourth stage is a little more difficult than the previous steps. When we experience pleasant physical feelings, joy and contentment, we are still in the realm of duality, namely there is the experience and also the experiencer, called "me," who enjoys his/her joyful situation. However, to be able to have utter peace and complete equanimity, the experiencer, namely "me," has to disappear and letting go of that is at first somewhat difficult. Meditators often feel a resistance in the mind at this stage to go further, because the fear of losing "control" arises.

At this point we need to remind ourselves that we have never been "in control." If we had been, we would certainly never have allowed unhappiness, fear or worry to arise, but would always have controlled our mind in such a way that it would only generate happiness. Yet, such has not been the case in anybody's experience. It follows, therefore, that only now are we learning control for the first time. This consideration may help to allay fear.

What is needed at this moment in the meditation is a soft and gentle surrender, a giving in and a giving up of all hopes, wishes, ideas and plans. Just relaxing into the soft, embracing stillness of a momentarily, completely pure mind.

Having been able to do that, the resulting intuitive understanding after the experience will show us that only without the "me" being in the act can we know total peace. This will certainly encourage a meditator to practise towards that goal with diligence, having known the momentary result of infinite surrender.

These are by no means "super-natural" achievements, since what our minds can do must be natural. But even more importantly, everyone's mind yearns for these states of joy and peace, and has a natural interest in and proclivity for them. Surely, that makes it quite clear that with training and instruction, it should be possible for anyone to have access to true meditation.

After having perfected access to all four stages of fine-material absorption, and being able to remain in them for as long as we wish, we are now ready to practise the four immaterial absorptions. Their name implies that they are of a finer substance than we have experienced until now and also that they concern mind-states, which are not even vaguely familiar to us. However our ability to enter and remain in the first four stages, make the following steps quite natural progression.

The fifth stage of absorption is called "infinite space" and it is surely not a common state of being for ordinary people. However, its unfathomable name need not deter us from practising and experiencing it.

116

Just as the first of the fine-material absorption was concerned with body feeling, likewise is the first of the immaterial absorptions, only on a more refined basis. While pleasant body feelings were centered on ourselves, infinite space is centered on totality of manifestation. For many meditators this begins with a feeling of expansion of their own body, so that it quickly loses all its outlines and there is no longer a feeling of a personal body. It is replaced by a feeling of infinite spaciousness in which no separate entities exist, least of all oneself. This state also contains utter peacefulness, since there is no one there to have any worries or fears.

Having been able to abide in this absorption leaves behind a clear knowing that our own personal body identity is a delusion, strictly a worldly convenience without truth behind it. From then on we will never look upon our own body with the same idea of ownership and identification as before, but will see it for what it is, namely a manifestation of our own craving, which is not desirable to perpetuate.

In the same way, as the next step in the fine-material absorptions was concerned with the mind, so the following stage of meditation in the immaterial realm is concerned with consciousness, pertaining to awareness. It begins with a feeling of expansion of our own mind till it breaks the boundaries of personalized awareness and merges with an infinity of consciousness.

Naturally, this state also contains complete and utter peacefulness since there is nothing and nobody to disturb it.

Just as the infinity of space leaves no doubt of the lack of a personal body identity, so does the infinity of consciousness remove our delusion of personalized mind

There are statements by Indian sages, such as "I am that" or "I am everything" and we may have thought this to be presumptuous. In reality it is a statement of just such experiences as described above, which leave no residue of personalized existence but only a merging into totality, into everything.

This step in the meditation leads to the next one, called "the base of nothingness." Contentment as the third step in the fine-material realm left nothing to be desired. Likewise in the sphere of nothingness we find nothing desirable. This comes about with the expansion of our consciousness into totality; we enter into a feeling of no-thing anywhere to be found, which is solid, unchanging, gives security or provides a hold which can be attached to or leaned upon. All, the whole universe, is in flux. This should not be confused with the misunderstanding that there is nothing in existence. There certainly are manifestations, but they contain nothing of intrinsic value and are in reality only particles of energy falling apart and coming together again.

Only the meditative experience with an expanded consciousness of such a universe can give us the inner vision of this truth and thereby change our outlook upon ourselves and our reactions to the world we experience.

In the fine-material absorptions the fourth stage is utter peace, which renews and refurbishes mental energy, lacks all distinctions and "me" concepts. In the immaterial realm, the fourth step is named "neither perception nor non-perception." This experience lacks awareness of anything, is completely restful, provides mental energy, makes a state of being possible where mental activity, even the most subtle, is suspended for a while, and paves the way for the "attainment of extinction," which is the prerogative of non-returners and enlightened ones.

It goes without saying that the ability to concentrate for extended periods of time automatically cuts down on our defilements, so that someone who meditates diligently and continuously can expect a gradual lessening of all negative characteristics and also their final elimination. Such a one can make an end to all craving and attain Nibbāna here and now.

Glossary

The following Pali words encompass concepts and levels of ideas for which there are no adequate synonyms in English. The explanations of these terms have been adapted from the *Buddhist Dictionary* by Nyanatiloka Mahāthera.

Anāgāmi Non-Returner. A noble disciple on the third stage of holiness who has no sensual desire.

Anatta No-self, non-ego, egolessness, impersonality; neither within the bodily and mental phenomena of existence, nor outside of them can be found anything that in the ultimate sense could be regarded as a self-existing real ego-identity, soul or any other abiding substance.

Anicca Impermanence, a basic feature of all conditioned phenomena, be they material or mental, coarse or subtle, one's own or external.

Anusaya The seven proclivities, inclinations or tendencies.

Arahat/Arahant The Holy One. Through the extinction of all cankers, he reaches already in this very life the deliverance of mind, the deliverance through wisdom, which is free from cankers, and which he himself has understood and realized.

Ariya Noble One, Noble Person.

Glossary

Avijjā Ignorance, nescience, unknowing, synonymous with delusion, is the primary root of all evil and suffering in the world, veiling man's mental eyes and preventing him from seeing the true nature of things.

Bhavarāga Craving for continued existence; one of the seven tendencies.

Cittaviveka Mental detachment, the inner detachment from sensuous things.

Deva Heavenly being, deity, god. A celestial being who lives in a happy worlds, but is not freed from the cycle of existence.

Dhamma The liberating law discovered and proclaimed by the Buddha, summed up in the Four Noble Truths. Also used, in lower case, as a mental object, such as a thought.

Diṭṭhi View, belief, speculative opinion. If not qualified by right, it mostly refers to wrong and evil view or opinion.

Dukkha (1) In common usage: pain, painful feeling, which may be bodily or mental.

(2) In Buddhist usage as, e.g. in the Four Noble Truths: suffering, ill, the unsatisfactory nature and general insecurity of all conditioned phenomena.

Jhāna Meditative absorptions. Tranquility meditation.

Kalyāṇamitta Noble or good friend. A senior monk who is the mentor and friend of his pupil, wishing for his welfare, concerned with his progress, and guiding his meditation; in particular the meditation teacher.

Kamma/Karma Action denotes the wholesome and unwholesome volitions and their concomitant mental factors, causing rebirth and shaping the character of beings and thereby their destiny. The term does not signify the result of actions and most certainly not the deterministic fate of man.

Kammaṭṭhāna lit.: working-ground (i.e., for meditation) is the term in the commentaries for subjects of meditation.

Kāya-viveka Bodily detachment, i.e. abiding in solitude free from alluring sensuous objects.

Khandha The five groups or aggregates. The five aspects in which the Buddha has summed up all the physical and mental phenomena of existence, and which appear to the ordinary man as his ego or personality, to wit: body, feeling, perception, mental formations and consciousness.

Lokiya Mundane, are all those states of consciousness and mental factors arising in the worldling, as well as in the noble one, which are not associated with the supermundane

Lokuttara Supermundane, is a term for the four paths and four fruitions.

Magga-phala Path and fruit. First arises the path consciousness, immediately followed by fruition, a moment of supermundane awareness.

Māna Conceit, pride, one of the ten fetters binding one to existence, also one of the underlying tendencies.

Māra The Buddhist tempter figure, the personification of evil and passions, of the totality of worldly existence and of death.

Mettā   Loving kindness, one of the four sublime emotions (*brahma-vihāra*).

Nibbāna   lit. Extinction, to cease blowing, to become extinguished. Nibbāna constitutes the highest and ultimate goal of all Buddhist aspirations, i.e., absolute extinction of that life-affirming will manifested as greed, hate and delusion and clinging to existence, thereby the absolute deliverance from all future rebirth.

Nīvaraṇa   Hindrances, five qualities which are obstacles to the mind and blind our mental vision, and obstruct concentration, to wit: sensual desire, ill-will, sloth and torpor, restlessness and worry, and sceptical doubt.

Papañca   Proliferation, elaboration, lit. expansion, diffuseness, development, manifoldness, multiplicity, differentiation.

Paṭiccasamuppāda   Dependent Origination is the doctrine of the conditionality of all physical and psychical phenomena.

Puthujjana   Worldling, lit. one of the many folk, ordinary man, anyone still possessed of all the ten fetters binding to the round of rebirths.

Sacca   Truth, such as the Four Noble Truths.

Sakadāgāmi   Once-returner. Having shed the five lower fetters, he reappears in a higher world to reach Nibbāna.

Sakkāya-diṭṭhi   Personality-belief is the first of the ten fetters and is abandoned at stream-entry.

Samatha   Tranquility, serenity, is a synonym of *samādhi* (concentration).

Saṃsāra   Round of rebirth, lit. perpetual wandering, is a name by which is designated the sea of life ever restlessly heaving up and down.

Sangha   lit. Congregation, the name for the community of monks and nuns. As the third of the Three Gems and the Three Refuges, it applies to the community of the Noble Ones.

Saṃvega   The sources of emotion, or a sense of urgency.

Saṅkhāra   Most general usage: formations. Mental formations and kamma formations. Sometimes: bodily functions or mental functions. Also: anything formed.

Sīlabbata-parāmāsa   Attachment to mere rules and rituals is the third fetter and one of the four kinds of clinging. It disappears on attaining to stream-entry.

Sotāpatti   Stream-entry, the first attainment of becoming a noble one.

Vicikicchā   Sceptical doubt is one of the five mental hindrances and one of the three fetters, which disappears forever at stream-entry

Vipassanā   Insight into the truth of the impermanence, suffering and impersonality of all corporal and mental phenomena of existence.

Yathā-bhūta-ñāṇa-dassana   The knowledge and vision according to reality. One of eighteen chief kinds of insight.

Of related interest from the BPS

Buddha, My Refuge
Contemplation of the Buddha based on the Pali Suttas
Bhikkhu Khantipālo
This book weaves together a rich variety of texts from the Pali Canon illustrating each of the Buddha's nine outstanding virtues. A beautiful and inspiring anthology.
BP 409, 2006, 134 pp.

The Way to Ultimate Calm
Selected Discourses
Webu Sayādaw
Contains eight full discourses by one of the greatest Burmese meditation masters of this century.
BP514, 2001, 199 pp.

Buddhist Dictionary
A Manual of Buddhist Terms and Doctrines
Nyanatiloka Mahāthera
Authentic, clear explanations of all key Theravada Buddhist terms and doctrines, arranged alphabetically, with textual references. An indispensable aid for the serious student of Theravada Buddhism.
BP 601, 2004, 272 pp.

Prices as in the latest BPS catalogue
(http://www.bps.lk)

The Buddhist Publication Society

The BPS is an approved charity dedicated to making known the Teaching of the Buddha, which has a vital message for all people.

Founded in 1958, the BPS has published a wide variety of books and booklets covering a great range of topics. Its publications include accurate annotated translations of the Buddha's discourses, standard reference works, as well as original contemporary expositions of Buddhist thought and practice. These works present Buddhism as it truly is—a dynamic force which has influenced receptive minds for the past 2500 years and is still as relevant today as it was when it first arose.

For more information about the BPS and our publications, please visit our website, or contact:

The Administrative Secretary
Buddhist Publication Society
P.O. Box 61
54 Sangharaja Mawatha
Kandy • Sri Lanka

E-mail: bps@bps.lk
Web site: http://www.bps.lk
Tel: 0094 81 223 7283 • Fax: 0094 81 222 3679